Albert Ellis Live!

I (Windy Dryden) dedicate this book to the one and only Albert Ellis on the occasion of his 90th birthday on 27 September 2003

Happy birthday, Albert, and many more!

Albert Ellis
Live!

WINDY DRYDEN
&
ALBERT ELLIS

SAGE Publications
London • Thousand Oaks • New Delhi

First published 2003

SAGE Publications Ltd
6 Bonhill Street
London EC2A 4PU

SAGE Publications Inc.
2455 Teller Road
Thousand Oaks, California 91320

SAGE Publications India Pvt Ltd
B-42, Panchsheel Enclave
Post Box 4109
New Delhi 100 017

British Library Cataloguing in Publication data

A catalogue record for this book is available from the British
Library

ISBN 0 7619 4342 0

Library of Congress Control Number: 2003102951

Typeset by C&M Digitals (P) Ltd, Chennai, India
Printed in Great Britain by TJ International Ltd, Padstow, Cornwall

Contents

Preface by Windy Dryden

Albert Ellis is the originator of Rational Emotive Behaviour Therapy, a leading cognitive-behavioural approach to counselling and psychotherapy. Ellis's practice of REBT spans a broad range of therapeutic contexts with a variety of client populations (Ellis & Dryden, 1997). While an in-depth analysis of his regular therapy practice has been published (Yankura & Dryden, 1990), to date no similar analysis of Ellis's work in demonstration sessions has been undertaken. This book seeks to provide such an examination.

A demonstration session is a single session of REBT undertaken with a volunteer client who understands the one-off nature of the interview. The purpose of the demonstration session is to help the person in the client role and to give the audience (who may be physically present or who may be absent but either watching a video or film of the session or listening to an audiotape of it) an opportunity to see or hear an REBT practitioner in action so that they can gain an understanding of how this therapeutic approach is practised. Albert Ellis has done very many demonstration sessions in the following contexts:

1 At the Friday Night workshop conducted at the Albert Ellis Institute where Ellis interviews two volunteers in front of an audience who later have an opportunity to ask both Ellis and the client questions (Dryden, Backx & Ellis, 2002). Ellis has been conducting the Friday Night workshop regularly since June 1965 and recent research testifies to the fact that the vast majority of volunteer clients find their interview with Ellis a constructive experience (Ellis & Joffe, 2002).

2 During professional training workshops internationally where Ellis interviews volunteer participants in front of their professional peers. Again, members of the audience have the opportunity to ask Ellis and the volunteer questions about the experience.

3 In videotapes and audiotapes for the professional community. Some of these tapes have been published by the Albert Ellis Institute while others have been made by or for the Institute for in-house training programmes, but have not been published. The five interviews that are presented and analysed in this book are examples of the latter. They were unpublished videotaped interviews that I transcribed for the purpose of writing this book.

The most famous of Ellis's demonstration sessions was made for the professional community. This was his interview with Gloria in the first of the *Three Approaches to Psychotherapy* films made by Everett

Shostrom (1965). Weinrach (1986) has reviewed Ellis's work with Gloria in this film which has both attracted people to REBT and turned others away from this therapeutic approach, perhaps in equal measure.

An Ellis demonstration session has a number of identifiable features that you will be able to discern in the interviews that follow:

- It is a single, one-off therapeutic encounter with a volunteer client.
- It is educational as well as therapeutic in nature in teaching both the client and the audience about how REBT approaches the assessment and treatment of common psychological problems.
- It deals with volunteer clients' problems in a fairly general way. Thus, some disputing of irrational beliefs is done, but not at length.
- Clients are given some guidance on how to put what they have learned into practice.
- Clients are not taught the skills of disputing irrational beliefs in any systematic way.

It is important that readers do not make unwarranted generalisations and assume that Ellis's performance in these sessions is truly representative of how he practises REBT in ongoing individual therapy sessions. Thus, in regular sessions, but not in demonstration sessions, Ellis has the time to:

- collect important biographical data;
- carry out a brief history of the clients' psychological problems and previous treatment experiences;
- assess treatment expectancies and correct any misconceptions;
- assess to what extent clients have a predisposition to psychological disturbance by enquiring about the mental health status of their parents, siblings and relatives;
- give clients important information about REBT and how it differs from other therapeutic approaches;
- undertake a more thorough assessment than is possible in demonstration sessions;
- spend more time teaching the ABCs of REBT than is possible in demonstration sessions;
- dispute clients' irrational beliefs more thoroughly than is possible in demonstration sessions;
- teach clients how to use relevant REBT skills and techniques;
- check previous homework assignments.

This list should be regarded as representative rather than exhaustive.

It is also important that readers do not assume that all REBT therapists practise REBT in the same way. As has been shown elsewhere (Dryden, 2002), the practice of REBT is varied, with different therapists practising REBT in their own idiosyncratic fashion.

This book is representative of Albert Ellis's work in demonstration sessions and as such it is an important contribution to the REBT literature.

In Chapter 1, I present some of the fundamental ideas of REBT theory and practice. This account is not designed to be comprehensive, but provides enough information for readers to make sense of the material that follows. Each interview is presented verbatim, with one exception: excessive verbal dysfluencies have been omitted. Then I present the interview again with an in-depth commentary on Ellis's work.

While this book is designed to celebrate Ellis's 90th birthday on 27 September 2003, it is not meant to be hagiographical in nature. Rather, it is intended to provide a balanced, honest, critical appraisal of Ellis's work in one-off demonstration sessions.

Windy Dryden
London & East Sussex

Preface by Albert Ellis

Windy Dryden has been a Rational Emotive Behaviour Therapy (REBT) practitioner for a quarter of a century and during that time he has seen hundreds of clients, given scores of talks and workshops and effectively taught and supervised numerous therapists and counsellors in their practice of REBT. In addition, he has written many papers and has published substantially more than my own 70 books. Finally, he has made a number of special contributions to the theory and practice of REBT that have significantly influenced many of its practitioners, including myself.

Albert Ellis Live! is one of the most original books on REBT ever published. It presents several verbatim transcripts of my demonstration sessions during which I show volunteers how they can use REBT to solve their emotional-behavioural problems. The sessions are similar to the somewhat famous Problems of Everyday Living sessions that I have been giving in public almost every Friday night in New York with volunteer clients from the audience. The sessions Windy includes in the present book are a little different from my Friday Night workshop sessions in that the clients in this book are somewhat more sophisticated than my Friday Night volunteer clients and at least two of them seem quite knowledgeable about REBT. In general my Friday Night volunteers know practically nothing about REBT: this helps to explain why with the clients in this book I more quickly present REBT solutions to them and why I only consider their primary problems (e.g. something they are anxious, depressed or angry about) rather than also deal with their secondary problems (e.g. their anxiety about their anxiety or their depression about their depression). At my Friday Night workshops, I almost always address their secondary problems, too.

I especially appreciate Windy's informative and interpretative comments on the specific points I address in these verbatim therapy sessions. He very clearly shows the reader how I usually conform to my own REBT theory in dealing with clients' problems. But he also shows them how sometimes I do not follow my own theory. At those times, Windy succinctly shows how he or another REBT practitioner might intervene differently than the way in which I intervene. I quite agree with Windy that some of his suggested interventions follow REBT theory and practice better than those I actually made with the client and that it might have been better if I had used some of them. I realise from reading Windy's analyses that I definitely did some things that perhaps I should not have done and that I also neglected to use some REBT points with my clients that I could have helpfully used. Windy shows me in his comments that none of us – including myself, the originator of REBT – is perfect. So I want to thank him for some of his suggested corrections to my therapeutic work. Live and learn!

This book can be of distinct value to readers who want to discover what REBT is and how to use it with their clients. It clearly states the fundamentals of REBT; shows how they can be used effectively in a single first session with a client; shows how even the best therapists can *improve* on their use of REBT; indicates precise ways of using its disputing techniques; and shows how it works as an excellent teaching device with receptive clients and with people who observe clients undergoing live demonstrations of REBT, such as those that are included in this book.

Albert Ellis Live! also suggests some research studies of the effectiveness of REBT. Thus, it gave me the idea that if live sessions, like those included in this book, were taped or videotaped, and if the clients who are interviewed agree to listen to their own tapes several times – say at least once a month for six months after they have had their live session – it might be ascertained whether they seemed to benefit from their single session (as did some of the participants who were interviewed after their demonstration session) and also whether they got the REBT therapeutic message on the tape recordings more strongly and more emotionally than they got those messages after having a single therapy session. Listening several times to tapes of their own sessions may help them achieve stronger 'emotional' than 'intellectual' insight than they would achieve when they just have a single live session. This is only a hypothesis of mine and it would be good to have it empirically tested.

Albert Ellis Live! is a most interesting and valuable addition to REBT literature. Read and see for yourself!

Albert Ellis PhD
Albert Ellis Institute
45 East 65th Street
New York NY 10021
USA

1

Rational Emotive Behaviour Therapy and Albert Ellis's Use of Demonstration Sessions
by Windy Dryden

Rational Emotive Behaviour Therapy (REBT) is an approach to counselling that can be placed firmly in the cognitive-behavioural tradition of psychotherapy, meaning that it particularly focuses on the way that we think and behave, in its attempt to understand our emotional responses. REBT was founded in 1955 by Dr Albert Ellis, an American clinical psychologist who brought together his interests in philosophy and psychology, which are still present in this approach over 45 years on. One of the hallmarks of REBT is that it holds that people can be taught and can learn the principles of good mental health. Albert Ellis has been conducting demonstration sessions of REBT for many years. These sessions have a triple purpose: (1) to teach volunteer clients how to understand and address their problems using REBT; (2) to show members of the audience how they might use REBT to understand and address their own problems and (3) to give therapists who are training in REBT or who have an interest in learning more about REBT a model of practice, and an expert one at that.

In this opening chapter I will discuss those theoretical and practical components of REBT that are particularly germane to understanding Albert Ellis's clinical behaviour in demonstration sessions of REBT.

The ABCDEs of REBT

REBT therapists employ an ABCDE framework in helping clients to understand and address their psychological problems. I will briefly present these components.

'A' = Activating event
Clients disturb themselves about key aspects of a situation. These aspects are known in REBT as activating events. In the following demonstration sessions, volunteers will discuss their disturbed feelings about failure, discomfort, disapproval and even about their own disturbed feelings. These are all activating events and are placed under 'A' in the ABCDE framework. When dealing with clients' disturbed feelings, we are primarily dealing with negative activating events or adversities.

'B' = Belief

It is a major premise of REBT that while our emotions are usually about activating events at 'A' these 'As' do not cause our emotional reactions. Rather, our emotions are primarily determined by the beliefs that we hold about the activating events.

'C' = Consequences of the beliefs at B about the activating event at A (there are three such consequences: emotional, behavioural and thinking)

When a client holds a belief about an activating event, she (in this case) will tend to experience an emotion, she will tend to act in a certain way and she will tend to think in certain ways. These three consequences of this A × B interaction are known as emotional, behavioural and thinking consequences respectively.

'D' = Disputing

In REBT we challenge or dispute our clients' irrational beliefs. Disputing can be cognitive, behavioural or emotive in nature and works best when all three are used in concert.

'E' = Effects of disputing

When disputing is successful, the client experiences a more constructive emotive, behavioural and cognitive effect about the activating event.

Rational Beliefs at B

REBT argues that there are four basic rational beliefs and that they have the following five major characteristics. They are:

(a) flexible or non-extreme
(b) conducive to your mental health and to productive interpersonal relationships
(c) helpful to you as you strive towards your goals
(d) true
(e) logical

Now let me discuss the four rational beliefs put forward by REBT theory.

Full preference

Human beings have desires, and for desires to be the cornerstone of healthy functioning, they take the form of a full preference. A full prefer-ence has two components. The first is called the asserted preference. Here you make clear to yourself what you want (either what you want to happen or exist or what you want not to happen or exist). The second component is called the 'negated demand'. Here you acknowledge that what you want to occur or exist does not have to occur or exist.

In short, we have:

> Full preference = 'asserted preference' component + 'negated demand' component

Non-awfulising belief

When your full preference is not met it is healthy for you to conclude that it is bad that you have not got what you wanted. It is not healthy to be indifferent about not getting what you desire. As with a full preference, a non-awfulising belief has two components. The first component may be called 'asserted badness'. Here you acknowledge that it is bad that you have not got what you want or that you have got what you don't want. The second component is called 'negated awfulising'. Here you acknowledge that while it is bad when you don't get your desires met it is not awful, terrible or the end of the world.

In short, we have:

> Non-awfulising belief = 'asserted badness' component + 'negated awfulising' component

High frustration tolerance (HFT) belief

When your full preference is not met it is healthy for you to conclude that it is difficult for you to tolerate not getting what you want, but that you can tolerate it. An HFT belief also has three components. The first component may be called 'asserted struggle' because you recognise that it is a struggle to put up with not getting what you want. The second component is called 'negated unbearability'. Here you acknowledge that while it is a struggle to tolerate not getting your desires met it is not intolerable. The third component is called the 'worth tolerating' component and points to the fact that not only can you tolerate not getting what you want, but it is worth doing so.

In short, we have:

> High frustration tolerance belief = 'asserted struggle' component + 'negated unbearability' component + 'worth tolerating' component

Acceptance belief

When your full preference is not met it is healthy for you to accept this state of affairs. There are three types of acceptance belief: a self-acceptance belief where you accept yourself for not meeting your desires or for not having them met; an other-acceptance belief where you accept another person or other people for not meeting your desires, and an acceptance of life conditions belief where you accept life conditions when they don't meet your desires.

There are three components to an acceptance belief which I will illustrate with reference to a self-acceptance belief. The first is called the 'negatively evaluated aspect' component. Here you recognise when you have not met your desires or that your desires have not been met by others or by life conditions and you evaluate this particular aspect negatively. The second is called the 'negated global negative evaluation' component. Here you acknowledge that while you may have acted badly, for example or experienced a bad event, the whole of you is not bad. The third is called the 'asserted complex fallibility' component. Whereas in the second component you negated the view that you are a bad person, for example, here you assert what you are: a complex fallible human being.

In short, we have:

Acceptance belief = 'negatively evaluated aspect' component + 'negated global negative evaluation' component + 'asserted complex fallibility' component

Irrational Beliefs at B

REBT argues that there are four basic irrational beliefs, which have the following five major characteristics:

(a)   rigid or extreme
(b)   conducive to psychological disturbance and impaired interpersonal relationships
(c)   unhelpful to you as you strive towards your goals
(d)   false
(e)   illogical

Now let me discuss the four irrational beliefs put forward by REBT theory.

Demand
REBT theory holds that when you take your desires and turn them into rigid demands, absolute necessities, musts, absolute shoulds and the like, you make yourself emotionally disturbed when you don't get what you believe you must. Even when you do get what you believe you must, you are still vulnerable to emotional disturbance when you hold a rigid demand at the point when you become aware that you might lose what you have and need.

A rigid demand has two components. The first is known as the asserted preference and is the same as the asserted preference component of a full preference. Again, you make clear to yourself what you want (either what you want to happen or exist or what you want not to happen or exist). The second component is called the 'asserted demand'. Here you take what you want and you turn it into a 'rigid demand' (e.g. 'I want to do well in my examination and therefore I have to do so').

In short, we have:

Rigid demand = 'asserted preference' component + 'asserted demand' component

Awfulising belief

When your rigid demand is not met then you will tend to reach the extreme conclusion that it is awful, horrible, terrible or the end of the world that you haven't got what you insist you must have. As with a non-awfulising belief, an awfulising belief, has two components. The first component is the same as that in the anti-awfulising belief – 'asserted badness'. Here you acknowledge that it is bad that you have not got what you want or that you have got what you don't want. The second component is called 'asserted awfulising'. Here you transform your non-extreme evaluation of badness into an extreme evaluation of horror (e.g. 'Because it would be bad if I were to fail my exam, it would be horrible were I to do so').

In short, we have:

> Awfulising belief = 'asserted badness' component + 'asserted awfulising' component

Low frustration tolerance (LFT) belief

When your rigid demand is not met, you will tend to reach the extreme conclusion that you cannot bear not getting what you demand. Unlike an HFT belief which has three components, an LFT belief tends to have only two. The first is again known as the 'asserted struggle' because you recognise that it is a struggle to put up with not getting what you must have. The second component is called 'asserted unbearability'. Here you acknowledge that it is not just a struggle to put up with not getting your demand met, it is intolerable. Since you think that you cannot put up with not getting your demand met, whether or not it is worth tolerating does not become an issue. You can't tolerate it and that's that.

In short, we have:

> Low frustration tolerance belief = 'asserted struggle' component + 'asserted unbearability' component

Depreciation belief

When your rigid demands are not met you will tend to depreciate yourself, depreciate others or depreciate life conditions. Thus, there are three types of depreciation belief: a self-depreciation belief where you depreciate yourself for not meeting your demands or for not having them met; an other-depreciation belief where you depreciate another person or other people for not meeting your demands and a depreciation of life conditions belief where you depreciate life conditions when they don't meet your demands.

There are two components to a depreciation belief which I will illustrate with reference to a self-depreciation belief. The first component is called the 'negatively evaluated aspect' component. Here you recognise when you have not met your demands or that your demands have not been met by others or by life conditions and you evaluate this particular aspect negatively. The second component is called 'asserted global negative evaluation'. Here you give yourself a global negative rating for not meeting your demands, for example. Thus, you may acknowledge that you have acted badly and then evaluate yourself as a bad person for acting badly.

In short, we have:

> Depreciation belief = 'negatively evaluated aspect' component + 'asserted global negative evaluation' component

As we shall see, when Ellis is disputing volunteer clients' demands he particularly helps them to distinguish between their full preferences and their demands but when he is disputing their other irrational beliefs, he tends not to be as systematic in helping them to distinguish these irrational beliefs from their rational alternatives.

Healthy and Unhealthy Negative Emotions at C

When a client's 'A' is negative and he (in this case) holds a set of rational beliefs at 'B' about this 'A', his emotional 'C' will be negative but healthy. Thus, when he faces a threat, it is healthy for him to feel concerned and when he has experienced a loss, it is healthy to feel sad. Other healthy negative emotions (so called because they feel unpleasant but help deal constructively with negative life events) are: remorse, disappointment, sorrow, healthy anger, healthy jealousy and healthy envy.

When a client's 'A' is negative, but this time he holds a set of irrational beliefs at 'B' about this 'A', his emotional 'C' will be negative and unhealthy. Thus, when he faces a threat, it is unhealthy to feel anxious and when he has experienced a loss, it is unhealthy to feel depressed. Other unhealthy negative emotions (so called because they feel unpleasant and they interfere with dealing constructively with negative life events) are: guilt, shame, hurt, unhealthy anger, unhealthy jealousy and unhealthy envy.

In his demonstration sessions, Ellis occasionally checks explicitly to see whether his client's negative emotion is unhealthy rather than healthy, but most often he assumes that a client's expressed negative emotion is unhealthy even if it is expressed in vague terms (e.g. 'upset') unless it is clear that it is not.

Constructive and Unconstructive Behaviour at C

When a client's 'A' is negative and he holds a set of rational beliefs at 'B' about this 'A', his behaviour at 'C' is likely to be constructive. Such behaviour is constructive in three ways. First, it will help the person change the negative event that he is facing if it can be changed. Second, it will help him to make a healthy adjustment if the event cannot be changed and third it will help him to go forward and make progress in achieving his goals.

When the client's 'A' is negative, but this time he holds a set of irrational beliefs at 'B' about this 'A', his behaviour at 'C' is likely to be unconstructive. Such behaviour is unconstructive in three ways. First, it won't help him to change the negative event that he is facing if it can be changed. Indeed, such unconstructive behaviour will often make a bad situation worse. Second, it will prevent him from making a healthy adjustment if the event cannot be changed and third it will take him away from pursuing his goals.

In his demonstration sessions, Ellis usually works with unhealthy emotional Cs, but occasionally (as in his interview with Yvonne) he does work with unproductive behaviour.

Productive and Unproductive Thinking at C

When the client's 'A' is negative and he holds a set of rational beliefs at 'B' about this 'A', his subsequent thinking (or thinking 'C') is likely to be productive. Such thinking is productive in two ways. First, it is realistic and allows the person to deal with probable outcomes. Second, it is balanced and enables him to recognise, for example that he will get a range of positive, neutral and negative responses to his behaviour. As a result these thinking 'Cs' enable him to respond constructively to realistically perceived situations.

When the client's 'A' is negative, but this time he holds a set of irrational beliefs at 'B' about this 'A', his subsequent thinking (or thinking 'C') is likely to be unproductive. Such thinking is unproductive in two ways. First, it is unrealistic in that he will tend to predict the occurrence of low probability, highly aversive outcomes. Second, it is skewed in that he thinks, for example, that most people will respond to him negatively, a few may respond to him neutrally but nobody will respond to him positively. As a result these thinking 'Cs' interfere with his ability to respond constructively to realistically perceived situations.

Ellis does not actively look for subsequent unproductive thinking in his demonstration sessions, but when volunteer clients reveal it, Ellis adopts the standard REBT approach and helps them to see that such thinking stems from their demands and other irrational beliefs and if Ellis is in the midst of a disputing sequence, he resumes disputing the client's irrational beliefs.

Ellis's Therapeutic Style

REBT practitioners generally adopt an active-directive therapeutic style. Ellis certainly does so, particularly in his demonstration sessions. He invariably adopts a problem-oriented stance at the very outset of each demonstration session presented and analysed in this book and all of his interventions are geared to helping his volunteer clients solve their emotional problems in a direct, focused manner.

His therapeutic style can also be characterised as that of an authoritative teacher in that he comes over as an expert teaching clients how they disturb themselves and what they can do to solve their emotional problems. In doing so, Ellis does not check out his clinical hunches as much as other REBT therapists might (Dryden, 2002). This probably stems from his clinical skill and the accuracy of his hunches as well as his adoption of the role of expert. Here as elsewhere Ellis is flexible and this can be seen in his interview with Yvonne (Chapters 10 and 11) where Ellis urges her not to accept what he says just because he says it, but to test it carefully against her experience.

In general, it is Ellis's high level of activity, his direction of the session and his unabashed adoption of the role of expert teacher that many practitioners from other therapeutic traditions particularly object to when they see Ellis's demonstrations or REBT. In addition, cognitive therapists criticise Ellis for his lack of collaboration with his volunteer clients. Ellis (1989) has written that full collaboration between client and therapist is disingenuous. He argues that REBT therapists know much more about how people disturb themselves and how they can un-disturb themselves and as such they need to take the lead in therapy and direct their clients' attention to how they particularly disturb themselves and how they can particularly un-disturb themselves. This 'taking the lead' attitude can be clearly seen in the demonstration sessions in this book. However, as can be seen in the two post-session interviews, the clients interviewed experienced Ellis as very understanding and helpful. This has been borne out in a research study of volunteer clients' experiences of the Friday Night workshop where 78 of 97 volunteers found their demonstration session with Albert Ellis 'very helpful' and the remaining 19 found it 'somewhat helpful'. None of research sample rated their session with Ellis as 'not helpful' (Ellis & Joffe, 2002).

What also emerges from Ellis's regular clients' and demonstration clients' accounts is that they do not experience him as particularly warm (DiGiuseppe, Leaf & Linscott, 1993). This is in line with Ellis's (1985) view that of all the core conditions put forward by Rogers (1957), therapist warmth is the least helpful and the most counter-therapeutic in that it may distract some clients from adopting a problem-solving approach to self-help and may reinforce an attitude of dire need for love and approval in others. While it is difficult to assess the presence or absence of warmth from the verbatim transcripts of the demonstration sessions presented here, the reader should be able to discern Ellis's warmth with Lucy when she was discussing the death of her daughter. This shows Ellis's flexibility in varying his therapeutic style according to what the client is discussing. Ellis's interview with Lucy also shows Ellis's flexibility in that he spends a good portion of the early part of this interview normalising and validating Lucy's feelings rather than disputing her irrational beliefs.

Assessment and Level of Specificity

Assessment in REBT takes place at three major levels. At the most general level, the REBT therapist gains a full picture of her (in this case) client's problems. This is usually done as therapy proceeds rather than at the outset of therapy before change-oriented interventions are used, but the latter does happen, and some REBT therapists do this when they are dealing with complex cases where they deem it important to gain an overall picture of their clients' problems before intervening in any one of them (Dryden, 1998a).

At the intermediate level, a full assessment is made of one of the client's problems, the one that she has chosen to focus on. This is known as the target problem in REBT. Here, the therapist carries out a cognitive-emotive-behavioural assessment of the client's target problem that is not limited to any specific example of the problem. Here, the therapist identifies the following:

1 a general recurring inferential theme (e.g. rejection or failure);
2 a general sense of the typical contexts in which these general inferential themes occurs (e.g. at work, in love relationships or with friends);
3 the client's most commonly experienced unhealthy negative emotions and/or behavioural responses and, less frequently, the thinking consequences of their irrational beliefs;
4 the client's general irrational beliefs that account for the responses outlined above;
5 the ways in which the client has attempted to deal with their problems.

At the most specific level of assessment, the REBT therapist encourages the client to identify and work with one example of their target problem. This may be a recent example, a typical example or a vivid example of the target problem and here the therapist endeavours to identify very specific information in the above five categories.

In the five demonstration sessions that follow, Ellis works most frequently at the intermediate level of assessment and his change-directed interviews continue at this intermediate level of specificity.

There are two major approaches to assessment of irrational beliefs in REBT: open-ended and theory-driven (DiGiuseppe, 1991a). In open-ended assessment of irrational beliefs, questions such as 'What are you telling yourself?' are asked. While these questions are informed by the general idea that thinking determines feelings, they are not informed by the specific REBT theory that irrational beliefs determine emotional problems. In theory-driven assessment of irrational beliefs, questions are informed by REBT theory such as 'What demand are you making?' When assessing irrational beliefs, Ellis frequently begins with open-ended questions and then follows these up with theory-driven didactic explanations. He rarely asks theory-driven questions.

Focus on Primary Emotional Problems versus Meta-emotional Problems

I have already made the point that Ellis is very problem oriented in the way he opens a demonstration session. 'What problem would you like to start with?' is a typical Ellis opening remark. The problem which the demonstration client chooses to work on is known as the target problem. This is typically a psychological problem in which the client experiences one or more unhealthy negative emotions or acts in a self-defeating manner. REBT therapists discourage clients from working initially with practical problems, preferring to start with their emotional problems about their problems. Most commonly when this is done successfully, clients often are able to solve their own practical problems since they are better able to think objectively about these problems. If they still require help with practical problem-solving their REBT therapist might outline a typical problem-solving sequence, teach them how to carry out a cost benefit analysis of their practical problem or suggest another person who has the necessary expertise in the area of their practical problem.

The emphasis in REBT is therefore very much on helping clients to solve their emotional problems. However, there are times when it is difficult for the therapist to do this because the client has an emotional problem about their emotional problem. I call this secondary emotional problem a meta-emotional problem and distinguish it from what is referred to in REBT theory as the primary emotional problem. REBT therapists differ from one another concerning their stance towards meta-emotional problems. Some tend always to assess for its presence and target it for change before the primary emotional problem if found. Others assess for it if it seems likely that it might exist and use a number of criteria for targeting it for change before the primary emotional problem. These therapists will work on the meta-emotional problem first if it is clear that its presence will interfere with work done on the primary emotional problem, if it is clinically more significant than the primary emotional problem and if the client can see the sense of working on it first. My experience is that the latter group of therapists are more likely to give clients a rationale for focusing on the meta-emotional problem first and to seek their agreement for so doing.

In the interviews that follow, it is clear that Ellis assesses for the presence of meta-emotional problems when he considers that they may exist and he unilaterally concentrates on them when he finds them, without any clearly stated rationale and certainly without seeking client agreement first. This is very much in keeping with Ellis's adoption of the position of authoritative teaching expert in his demonstration sessions.

Dealing with As

Clients often disturb themselves about events that seem phenomenologically accurate to them, but are probably distorted in reality. A major difference between REBT and other approaches to cognitive-behavioural therapy lies in the latter's stance to dealing with distorted inferences at A. Thus,

REBT therapists are less likely than their CBT colleagues to challenge distorted As at the outset. Rather, they will encourage clients to assume temporarily that A is correct in order to get to what they consider to be the source of their clients' disturbance – their irrational beliefs. This is apparent in the demonstrations presented and analysed here, as is Ellis's frequent reiteration that in taking this stance he is not condoning A if it transpires to be accurate and when it represents bad behaviour in others.

Not Making Explicit the iB-Connection

In working with clients in the assessment phase, REBT therapists usually make explicit for clients the relationship between their disturbed reactions at C and their irrational beliefs (iBs) at B. Here they stress that A does not cause C; rather C is largely determined by B. This is known in REBT as making explicit the iB–C connection. Ellis tends not to make this connection explicit. Instead, once he has assessed A and C, Ellis asks the client what she (in this case) is telling herself and once he has helped the client to identify an irrational belief, he moves on immediately to disputing it. Why does Ellis not explicitly make the iB–C connection? My view is that he does not do this either because he assumes that the client understands this connection without him having to make it explicit or because he thinks she will come to understand it through repetition of this point throughout the session.

Disputing

Disputing irrational beliefs is a key task of REBT therapists and Ellis's demonstration sessions clearly feature this task. DiGiuseppe (1991b) analysed Ellis's regular therapy sessions and showed that Ellis uses a number of disputing styles and three main questions while disputing. The main disputing styles featured in Ellis's work in these demonstration sessions are Socratic and didactic. In Socratic disputing of irrational beliefs, the therapist asks the client questions designed to encourage the client to think about whether her irrational beliefs are irrational or rational. Rather than didactically correct the client's incorrect answers, the therapist follows up with supplementary questions until the client understands the irrationality of her irrational belief and the rationality of her rational belief. In didactic disputing the therapist explains to the client why her irrational belief is irrational and why her rational belief is rational. Usually, REBT therapists use a combination of these two styles. In the demonstration sessions that follow, Ellis's most frequently employed disputing strategy is a didactic assertion that a rational belief is rational; he then asks the client Socratically for the reason why this is the case. If the client does not answer correctly, Ellis will provide it didactically rather than continue with a Socratic sequence. He does so because time is limited in a demonstration session and to persist with a Socratic sequence for too long would not be an efficient use of time.

In his regular therapy sessions, Ellis employs empirical (e.g. 'Is it true that you must do well?'), logical ('Does it logically follow that because you want to do well, you have to?') and pragmatic ('What are the consequences of believing that you must do well?') questions or didactic equivalents, although research has not been carried out to determine in which proportions he employs these different arguments. In the demonstration sessions that follow, Ellis uses empirical arguments most often.

Whether because time is pressing in demonstration sessions or because in authoritative mode he does not see the value of doing so, Ellis does not explain to his clients why he is going to dispute their irrational beliefs nor does he prepare them for disputing. As soon as the client articulates a relevant irrational belief, Ellis proceeds to dispute it.

Finally, in these demonstration sessions, Ellis uses disputing illustratively rather than fully. He wants to give his clients a taste of how to dispute a number of their irrational beliefs rather than concentrate on any one. Nor does he spend any time training clients to dispute their own irrational beliefs (Dryden, 2001), again probably because he does not think this is a good use of demonstration time.

The Insight Problem

About 40 years ago, Ellis (1963) wrote a paper distinguishing between two types of insight in REBT: intellectual insight (which is defined as a rational belief, lightly and occasionally held, which is rarely acted on and which does not lead to healthy emotions based on firmly held rational beliefs) and emotional insight (which is defined as a firmly held conviction in a rational belief, frequently acted on and which does lead to healthy emotions). The main task in therapy is to help clients go from intellectual to emotional insight. Obviously, in his demonstration sessions, Ellis cannot foster emotional insight in his volunteer clients given the one-off nature of such sessions. However, he does address this issue and shows clients what they need to do to achieve emotional insight, and he does teach some of them one or two techniques which with continued use can foster the development of emotional insight into rational beliefs.

Nature versus Nurture and the Human Condition

Ellis holds that people bring their tendencies to disturb themselves to situations and are not made disturbed by these situations. His view thus gives more weight to nature rather than to nurture in the acquisition of psychological disturbance. He also holds that while humans easily disturb themselves (some more easily than others, to be sure), change is possible through the ongoing application of cognitive, emotive and behavioural methods. One might think that in the time-sensitive context of a demonstration session Ellis would not expound on the issue of nature versus nurture and the human condition with respect to psychological disturbance, but he does do this. Most of the time when he does this it is in response to something that the client has said (normally some version of the view that their social environment taught them to be disturbed), but occasionally he may introduce the subject himself. It seems to me that Ellis does this because he sees the demonstration session as an opportunity to broadly educate the client and any watching audience (NB: none of these sessions were conducted in front of an audience) in the REBT model of psychological disturbance and change and simultaneously to debunk psychoanalytic and social learning theories of the same phenomena.

Use of Techniques in Demonstration Sessions

Due to the one-off nature of a demonstration session, Ellis uses a fairly restricted number of techniques. Apart from the assessment and disputing techniques which I have already discussed, Ellis uses the following two techniques most frequently: rational-emotive imagery and cognitive-behavioural homework assignments.

Rational-emotive imagery

Rational-emotive imagery (REI) is an emotive technique which Ellis uses after he has done some cognitive disputing of his volunteer client's irrational beliefs. REI gives the client practice at generating and staying with a rational alternative to her irrational belief while engaging her emotions. As such, it is a powerful technique that helps the client to develop emotional insight into her rational belief. The following set of instructions details Ellis's usual way of employing REI.

1   Take a situation in which you disturbed yourself and identify the aspect of the situation you were most disturbed about (A).
2   Close your eyes and imagine the situation as vividly as possible and focus on the A. Allow yourself to really experience the unhealthy negative emotion that you felt at the time, while still focusing intently on the A.
3   Really experience this disturbed emotion for a moment or two and then change your emotional response to a healthy negative emotion. All the time focus intently on the A. Do not change the intensity of the emotion, just the emotion. Keep experiencing this new emotion, all the time focusing on the A. If you go back to the old, unhealthy negative emotion, bring the new healthy negative emotion back.
4   When you have changed your emotion, open your eyes and ask yourself how you changed your emotion.
5   Make sure that you changed your emotional response by changing your specific unhealthy belief to its healthy alternative. If you did not do so, do the exercise again and keep doing this until you have changed your emotion only by changing your specific unhealthy belief to its healthy alternative.

After Ellis has taken the client through REI in the session, he suggests that she practise it daily as a homework assignment. In case the client does not do this he suggests the use of rewards and penalties where the client withholds a reward until she has done REI and implements a penalty if she fails to practise this technique for homework.

Cognitive-behavioural homework assignments

Cognitive-behavioural homework assignments arise out of the work that Ellis has done with clients during the sessions. They normally involve the client rehearsing a rational belief while acting consistently with it. Such assignments may involve an element of risk-taking and engage the client's emotions and are typified by shame-attacking assignments. Ellis particularly suggests shame-attacking assignments to clients when he has been working with them on their self-depreciation problems when these have an interpersonal context. The two main components of a shame-attacking exercise are as follows:

- The client carries out an activity in public that is designed to attract negative attention from others without alarming the public or without getting the client into trouble (e.g. wearing odd shoes or – Ellis's favourite – taking a banana out for a walk and feeding it to another banana!). The goal is for people to depreciate the client in some way in their minds, e.g. they think that the client is a strange person.
- The client accepts herself as a fallible human being who is acting strangely, but is not a strange person even if the watching public thinks that she is.

Some clients find the idea of doing shame-attacking exercises appealing while others are sceptical (see Ellis's interview with Fiona).

Giving Clients Tapes of Demonstration Sessions

Ellis sees demonstration sessions as educational as well as therapeutic in nature. Particularly in his Friday Night workshops, he gives volunteers a tape of the interview to take home and review. Reviewing the tape of the demonstration session at a later date, and several times if necessary, gives clients the opportunity to process the points covered in the session at their own speed. It is not clear from the information to hand whether the five clients received tapes of their session or not. What is clear is that the sessions were videotaped (although not in front of an audience) in 1982 and were designed to be used for professional training purposes at the Albert Ellis Institute. They were not, however, put on more general release within the wider professional community.

As I said in the preface, in the chapters that follow I present each interview in its entirety without comment. I then give an in-depth commentary on the interview, showing what I think Ellis is doing at various junctures.

2

Ellis's Interview with Fiona

Ellis: Fiona, what problem would you mainly like to talk about today?

Fiona: Actually I would like to just express my feelings about myself and what is going on in my life that I can't seem to cope with.

Ellis: Yeah sure, especially what you can't seem to cope with then I'll see if we can give you some ideas on how to cope with what you presumably can't cope with.

Fiona: That would be terrific. Um...basically I would say my whole life has been a roller-coaster but it's much heavier at this point in my life...my feelings of anger towards the world and with that anger also goes a feeling of self-pity and despair. It kind of changes from that, in other words I don't want to feel angry and I don't know how to express my anger so I hold it inside of me and I take it and turn it around and hurt myself.

Ellis: Yeah, well let me just see if I understand that. [*Fiona*: OK] I think you are saying that you have two feelings – one is that you feel very angry and you don't like that feeling, you don't want to feel that way but then you are also saying you feel like expressing the anger and you believe that if you express it, you will get it out and then it will go, but, since you don't express it, you then may put yourself down for not expressing it – is that correct?

Fiona: Yes, so I'm angry at myself for not expressing it but I am also terrified of feeling and showing that anger because I don't know if I can control it. [*Ellis*: Right] Anger frightens me. It's been part of my life...I can't even handle yelling, it's just terrifying, it's hurt my whole life, it's hurt my marriages, my relationships with friends and family and...I would like to have a healthy attitude in terms of my feelings with anger because I end up hurting myself all the time. [*Ellis*: Right] It doesn't accomplish anything in my life [*Ellis*: Right] and it also reflects itself in my professional life. I can't seem to stay in one career and work where I can...at my age, I'm 36, I want to feel successful, I want to have a successful life...and really...

Ellis: But as I see it, and again you correct me if I'm wrong, you have two levels: first the anger, which you are afraid might be really terrific and outstanding and overwhelm you, but then you are terrified about the anger [*Fiona*: Absolutely] because it knocks you off – is that right? [*Fiona*: …Mm hmm] Why don't we start with the second one then we'll get back to the anger itself, but let's just talk about it first, if you want to, the terror about the anger. Do you want to start there and then we'll get back to the anger itself?

Fiona: The terror, since I've never been angry in my life I can only assume what I am going to feel and that is out of control.

Ellis: Well, let's just assume the worst there, that you did, that you let yourself go on one occasion or a few occasions and you felt out of control, let's just suppose that, you got beyond yourself and you felt out of control. Now what are you afraid would happen then? Can you picture that out of controlledness and…?

Fiona: Yeah, I see myself shaking, I see myself…quivering. I see myself possibly killing – I don't know, it gets…I can't go that far with it [*Ellis*: Right] and I also see someone not liking me.

Ellis: Right. All right then let's just picture yourself shaking and quivering and feeling really murderous and somebody watching you or several people watching you and not liking you. Now, why would that be horrible if that were so, because we're deliberately now assuming the worst so to get you to see that even if you did express this anger it might not be the end of the world, but why would that be horrible if you expressed it, you got out of control *and* somebody or several people really disliked you?

Fiona: I really wouldn't know how to handle it, I wouldn't know how to…I can't handle people not liking me, it's…

Ellis: Because you feel *what*? When people don't like you, what's your own feeling? Let's suppose people don't like you and that's especially because you are really out of control, you're angry, then how do you feel…?

Fiona: Then I feel they'll see me for who I am.

Ellis: And now let's suppose now that…

Fiona: They're seeing a horrible person.

Ellis: All right now you prove to me that you are a horrible person if you're out of control and if people don't like you, how does that make you a horrible person?

Fiona: It's hard to answer that, you know…that's the whole problem.

Ellis: I know, but if we can get you to see that you are *not* a horrible person – you are a person *who* is acting, we'll say badly, very angrily out of control and unloved in this instance, then we'll solve maybe the most important part of your whole problem. But just think about that, you're out of control and people are *hating* you for being out of control. They are thinking you're a twerp, you're no good and you're really an impossible person. Now how does that make *you* no good?

Fiona: Well actually it doesn't, it probably is the reverse, it would be good for me to be that way because it's healthy.

Ellis: Well, you're thinking that's healthy, that doesn't have to be…

Fiona: Healthy, meaning I can't be a smiling, lovely person all the time.

Ellis: That's right. I don't think personally from our standpoint in Rational Emotive Behaviour Therapy that it's really healthy to be angry, but it's healthy to be assertive, to be yourself [*Fiona*: That's it exactly] and if you were yourself and … [*Fiona*: I'd feel damned good] Right, but now let's suppose you're not just assertive, you're horribly angry. [*Fiona*: I'm horribly angry] You're getting upset about it. Now again why would you have to put *you* down – not the out of control down because that wouldn't be so good. Now why would you have to put you as a human down if that were so?

Fiona: Because it would reinforce what I think of myself.

Ellis: And why do you think so badly of yourself?

Fiona: That goes back too long – it's too deep…it's too deeply embedded in me.

Ellis: Well I don't happen to think so. In Rational Emotive Behaviour Therapy we say that it does go back and you probably felt this way right from the beginning from age two, three or four because even then you had a certain implicit philosophy which you brought to any situation [*Fiona*: Correct] and that philosophy, do you know what that probably was, even at two, three, four and five?

Fiona: I was a brat. [*Ellis*: Right] I provoked my father who *was* an angry person [*Ellis*: Right] and only because I wanted him to show me his love [*Ellis*: Right] but instead I didn't know how to handle him, I didn't understand what was going on, I would provoke him to get his attention and he would hit me.

Ellis: All right, but you see you first provoked him to show his love. Now your philosophy behind that in regard to your being loved, what do you think that might have been?

Fiona: My philosophy then was to get his love, his attention [*Ellis*: Right] but it never worked that way.

Ellis: But was it just a desire or was it a *need*?

Fiona: It was a need [*Ellis* (*exaggerates*): Ahhh!] an absolute need.

Ellis: And that's what you brought to the situation at two, three, four, five, six. You had a dire *need*, necessity, for love and then you did anything – even acted brattily, did anything even against this father who was very angry himself. So your first philosophy that I see was a dire need for love, which incidentally I see you still having [*Fiona*: Absolutely] and that's why you did that.

   But then there was a second philosophy which was probably there too; along with the dire need for love, and I'm just going to take a guess about it now – and you check me – that I *have* to act well, I *have* to do the right thing *AND* therefore be approved – is that possible, that you've always had that kind of philosophy?

Fiona: Yeah I had to be the nice sweet little Fiona. [*Ellis*: Right] People would like me and think what a nice little girl.

Ellis: But do you see the contradiction right from the start?

Fiona: I was rebelling against…

Ellis: That's a little later, first I have to be myself and win love, and almost every child wants to win love and be approved especially by her father, mother and people like that, but instead of I'd like to, I *have* to. And then when I'm not loved I'll do almost anything because I *have* to do well and *have* to be loved and I'll even rebel. I need: (1) the attention, love – but (2) *I* need to express myself even when it gets me into trouble – isn't that what you felt as a child? – and don't you still feel a lot of that conflict that…

Fiona: Absolutely. I mean I did the same provocation in my marriage [*Ellis*: Yeah?] because I could not believe that this man could really love me and I had to test him all the time until he…er…he couldn't take it any longer.

Ellis: So we're right back to I need, I absolutely must have his love and then I will even go to extremes and test people [*Fiona*: It's very frightening] and then when they fail the test and don't love you that much, how do you feel about them?

Fiona: Exactly; how do I feel about them?

Ellis: When you've tested your husband's love or your father's love and they failed and they didn't really love you as much as you thought they should…

Fiona: Then it actually…what it was doing was reinforcing the fact that I'm not a good person.

Ellis: Ah reinforcing in your philosophy [*Fiona*: Yes] 'cos I *must* be loved and I *must* do well.

    [*Ellis raps his fist against his hand to emphasise the word 'must'.*]

Fiona: He promised he would love me for ever, my father supposedly should have loved me no matter what and he didn't.

Ellis: Because he's my father?

Fiona: Because he's my father.

Ellis: Right, and my husband because he's my husband?

Fiona: Yes – and because he promised me that he'd love me for ever, but he didn't.

Ellis: And therefore what did that make him and them who promised to love you for ever and don't go through with it? What do you think about them…temporarily…when you need this love?

Fiona: I didn't think of them, I just thought of me in terms of they're right, I'm a terrible person.

Ellis: That's one thing [*Fiona*: I put it all on me] but now let's get to the anger, did you also at times, not all the time, hate *them* for not giving you the love that you thought you needed?

Fiona: Of course I did.

Ellis: Ah – you see now that's two things. We start with *I* need the love, *I* should do the right thing and isn't it terrible, I'm an awful person when I don't, but then they should *see* my neediness and they should give in to it and they're terrible people. And then finally, or maybe not even finally, you add to that now I see I'm angry at the people I love and they love me less and isn't it horrible to be out of control and so brattish and so angry and you go right back to putting yourself down – isn't that right? [*Fiona*: Correct] Right.

Now let's unravel a couple of these things and show you what to do because I think it's very complicated – actually we've done it very, very briefly so you think a lot more about this – but I think it starts with a need to do well and be loved yourself. Then you get upset, self-downing, then you get angry at them for not giving it, then you get angry at you for being angry at them and maybe losing control, being brattish. But let's just take one of these things again, get back to that – the fundamental need to be loved, to do well with others. Now I'm not going to by any means debate or dispute your desire because everybody desires love. It's one of the most fine, the greatest things in the world, it really makes for relating, but you from the start and right now *have* to be loved and you *need* to be loved and you're viewing yourself as a terrible person when you're not. Now why *must* you be loved, not why do you desire it, why do you *have* to be…?

Fiona: It's an interesting point um…throughout my life it's always been, life was, I never was myself in terms of…I never knew who I was because I was always going by the standards of what their expectations for me were.

Ellis: Right or what you thought their expectations were.

Fiona: Or what I thought their expectations were [*Ellis*: Right] and primarily it seemed that I…er…I had to be married you know [*Ellis*: Right] in a very secure situation…so that's how I based my life…not in terms of what was expected of me.

Ellis: Right. To be a good person I had to fulfil what *they* expected of me.

Fiona: So I've never really done anything for me. I really never found out what I really need.

Ellis: Well, how can you when you're fundamentally…

Fiona: I couldn't and at this time of my life I'm trying to. So what I've done is eliminated love completely from my life, in fact people. I'm totally alone now.

Ellis: But that throws out the baby with the bathwater. Now suppose we could get you to see that you don't *need* love, it's very desirable, but you don't *need* it and you don't *have to* conform to what other people say you *should* conform to, though it would be nice if they did care for you, and then you would be able to risk getting involved if you really got rid of that *dire* necessity for doing the right thing and being loved. Now how could that be done? How could any human, you included, get rid of not the desire, we're not trying to get rid of that, 'cos you've really thrown out the baby with the bathwater, the desire. [*Fiona*: At this point, yes] How can you keep the desire to be loved, to be approved, to get along with others, to relate and *not* the necessity, the dire need that puts you down. How could you do that?

Fiona: Well, I think becoming my own person, number one.

Ellis: That would be one. That's excellent because then you see you'd risk being *you* and your philosophy would be 'I'm going to be me at all costs' and [*Fiona*: Right] and *if* they don't love me what could you conclude? They don't love me when I'm me. What could you conclude about that?

Fiona: Well, it's not that I'm a bad person though [*Ellis*: Right] because I'm happy with me [*Ellis*: Right] which is something I'm trying to work on.

Ellis: Right. You could conclude: 'Maybe it's too bad, I would wish they would like me as me and there must be somebody in the universe who would like me as me, you see, but they don't *have* to' – it's the necessity, [*pounds for emphasis*] the *demand* that does it not the desire. Now if you could really work on that 'I'd like to be me' primarily and then secondarily get those people to care for me who will accept me as *ME*. Wouldn't that solve a great deal of the problem?

Fiona: Yes, because I think at that point – if it should ever happen again – um…it would be a healthy relationship [*Ellis*: Right] it would not be that neurotic need and that provocation and that anger.

Ellis: And you've already implied from what you said a couple of minutes ago – the active solution, because if you would change your philosophy to 'I'm primarily going to be me and if they like me, great, but if they don't like me I can still accept myself as me', that would be fine if you thought that way, but one way to think that way is what you said 'to take risks' and what you might try are some of our shame-attacking exercises. Do you know anything about those?

Fiona: No, I've no idea.

Ellis: Well, you think of something that you consider shameful to do in public, in front of people, now not to hurt anybody, we don't want you to slap anybody in the face or get arrested – walk naked, you could walk naked in a public square and that would be shameful – but something like not tipping a waiter or taxi-cab driver. [*Fiona (laughs)*: Oh I do that] Well, that's not it then…or buy an outlandish costume dress and then never wearing it because you're ashamed to. [*Fiona*: Because of the shame] Yeah, you need something that you consider shameful. We get people to do foolish things, we get them to go on the New York subway, for example, and yell out the stops '42nd STREET' at the top of their lungs and to stay on the train you see. Or to go to Macy's or Bloomingdale's and yell out the time '11.50 AND A THIRD' and to stand there with everybody looking at them. Or to take a banana and a long leash and to walk the banana and take another banana and feed the first banana – to do foolish things. In public you can go right out on the street and stop somebody and say 'I just got out of the loony-bin what day is it?'

Fiona: Well, what purpose will that serve? [*Ellis*: The purpose is that you can pick something] – that this is what I'm doing and I don't care about the rest of the world?

Ellis: Well, to pick something that *you* consider shameful. Not that I do and to do it in public that's the first part, not get arrested, not get in trouble and then as you do it in public to work on not feeling ashamed, because shame is the essence of self-downing, of self-hatred. You see and if you can do these things in public and really not feel ashamed because *you* know why you're doing them, you know you're doing them for you, you know in this case they're even therapeutic, then that kind of thing helps you to resist the pressure which people have put on you since early childhood – and always will – and stops you from downing yourself.

Fiona: But why does it have to be something so absurd?

Ellis: Well, it doesn't. I'm just saying…actually it would be better if you pick something that you are normally ashamed to do and would be helpful for you…

Fiona: Yeah…like…like getting angry.

Ellis: That's right, you could do that…

Fiona: Like screaming at someone.

Ellis: That's right, you could deliberately scream. You'd pick somebody that's not too vulnerable – because we don't want you to hurt them – we don't want you to pick a little child or something like that, but somebody that you could get temporarily angry towards – scream at them, because you feel ashamed, not feel ashamed and then later show them why you did it, you see because we don't want anybody else to be hurt in the process. Or something else where you would really be thoroughly ashamed to do it, to risk it because all your life you have avoided this risk, you've sat on your feelings, you've sat on your anger, you've sat on everything and avoided it. Now if we can get you to do it and not put yourself down, not feel ashamed, that would be a long way towards solving your problems. You see. Then you could look at your anger, when you feel angry inside and you feel enraged with

	people and also acknowledge that you're creating the anger, do you know why you are creating the anger?
Fiona:	Can you repeat that last…?
Ellis:	When, let's suppose, …give me an instance recently where you got angry at somebody, you got very angry…you just felt it, not that you expressed it.
Fiona:	I don't express it. Um…Someone I work with…she…er…everything goes right for her…she gets all the great accounts, she gets dates, she gets roses sent to her every day, and I sit there and my stomach is in knots and I feel like saying – and then she complains…'Oh'…'Ooh'…You know she's just a spoilt person who has no true values, she's not sensitive and caring and she…everything good happens to her and I hate her. [*Ellis*: All right] and I get very angry because she hurt me as well.
Ellis:	Right…so at (A) an Activating Event in the ABCs of REBT, she acts this way and let's suppose she's doing you in and she's acting badly, and she's a spoilt brat herself. Let's assume that. [*Fiona*: This is her] Exactly. And at (C) a Consequence in your gut, you're feeling enraged, you're not doing anything about it. No…but you're feeling enraged. Now in Rational Emotive Behaviour Therapy we think that you're making yourself enraged. She is not enraging you…
Fiona:	You are right about that. [*Ellis*: Right, so what are you doing?] No one else is being annoyed by her.
Ellis:	That's exactly the point. [*Fiona*: Only I] Right so at (B), your Belief System, you are telling yourself something about her that is making you angry and I could guess from our theory, our ABC theory, what it is – but let's see if you could figure it out. What are you saying whenever you are angry at her?
Fiona:	Oh I know what I'm saying. [*Ellis*: What?] She doesn't deserve it, why her? [*Ellis*: Why her?] Why her? I'm working so much harder and I have had so many more problems in my life, why is everything good happening to her [*Ellis*: As?] she doesn't deserve it…
Ellis:	Right and she *shouldn't* be getting away with this. That's what I hear. [*Fiona*: Right] All right, now we ask in REBT – we go to (D), Disputing: Why *shouldn't* [*pounds for emphasis*] she act that way and get away with it? Why must she act well?
Fiona:	There is no why, there is no reason why she should do anything.
Ellis:	That's right. Now if you really believe that, you believe it at this second, then you would be sorry and displeased and annoyed at her behaviour, but you wouldn't be upset and angry at her. If you really believe she *should* act the way she does because she does…
Fiona:	Not that she should, I mean this is a person, her own personality, and her own whatever…um…I can't have her feel or think the

way I do [*Ellis*: Right] but it does upset me to think she's intelligent enough that she should be able to see it and she doesn't…

Ellis: But I say she shouldn't be able to see it. [*Fiona*: I understand that] Do you know why she shouldn't be able – even though she's intelligent – why should she act the way she does? Do you know why she should?

Fiona: She shouldn't…

Ellis: No, she should.

Fiona: Oh why she should act the way she is – [*Ellis*: Badly] because this is her.

Ellis: That's her nature…Right. [*Fiona*: That's right] Now whenever we're angry we're denying the nature of others. Now I'm not saying it's good that she acts that way, I'm assuming with you, it's bad, obnoxious, annoying that she should act annoyingly if that's her nature to act annoyingly.

Fiona: Just as I should get angry if that's how I feel…

Ellis: That's exactly right. Now it's not good that she acts that way nor even that you get angry. You'd better be *assertive* [*pounds for emphasis*] without anger, because anger is a damnation of her, you're damning her for her act, and if you're wise you'll say: 'Damnit I don't like what she is doing, I wish she wouldn't, and I'll probably tell her one of these days about it and try to get her to change.'

Fiona: Oh I would love to, that would be a very good step in the right direction.

Ellis: Right, but if we got you un-angry but still displeased with her behaviour and then assertive and we got you to not down yourself in case she and other people came back [*pounds for emphasis*] at you when you're assertive, wouldn't that solve the problem?

Fiona: It would certainly help.

Ellis: Right, then the thing to do, and you can do it in both orders, you can work on the anger first or the self-downing, the shame and determine that hereafter whenever things like this happen with people like her – and she's just an example, there are thousands of them – I will always think my thoughts and accept my thoughts and my feelings about her and even if she learns about my feelings, because I may tell her, and she puts me down I will accept myself no matter what she and other people think. [*Fiona*: I see] You see, I won't say I'm right, because I may be wrong, but even when I'm *wrong* I'll accept myself, because I am I and I have the right to be wrong. Now I'll try to be correct, but I don't *have* to be correct, I don't *have* to be approved by them you see…Then secondly – now that I'm ready to accept myself, I'll see that (1) I am displeased by her behaviour, but (2) I am damning her, I'm saying she *must* not do what she is indubitably doing and she *must* do it right now because that's the way she is right now, I wish she wouldn't and therefore I will assert myself and take the risk she won't love me, she won't like me at all, but she doesn't *have to* change, it is just highly desirable. D'you see?

Fiona: Absolutely.

Ellis: Now if we can get you to work along that line – on mainly your self-downing because I still think that's your biggest problem…and incidentally we'll go to one other thing and that is: let's suppose now that you're trying to work along the lines we're saying and you still run away, you still don't assert yourself and you don't go for yourself, and you run away and you avoid the situation, you cop out et cetera. Now again at (A), Activating Event, you're copping out, you're not expressing yourself, you're not being yourself. At (B), Belief System, you're telling yourself something which we'll get back to in a second and then at (C), you're feeling ashamed of your own copping out, because at (B) what are you saying again about *you* for copping out, for not expressing your feelings?

Fiona: I'm feeling angry…[*Ellis*: Right] I'm feeling the anger.

Ellis: Right, but what are you saying about not expressing feelings and copping out and running out of the situation and withdrawing? What are you saying about *you*, you know you're angry, you know you're non-assertive and you're not doing anything, now what are you telling yourself about your behaviour of copping out?

Fiona: At that point?

Ellis: Yeah, when you notice that you've copped out and not said anything.

Fiona: Well, let's see…I can't really verbalise it…

Ellis: Well, you're not liking yourself are you? [*Fiona*: No, I know that]…so you're saying, I copped out…

Fiona: I'm er…I'm that bad person again. [*Ellis*: That's right] I'm that stupid person, I'm that incompetent person, that child, whatever…

Ellis: That's right. Now you see the vicious circle, you began with self-downing to begin with and that's probably why you didn't speak up. You made yourself very angry. Then you were non-assertive about your feelings and on both levels the original one to down yourself and not speak up and then you blame yourself for not speaking up, so you do a double whammy. [*Fiona (laughs)*: It's a vicious circle, right] Right, you see. Now I say that if you start at the end again and say to yourself – 'Yes I didn't express myself, that was foolish because I would like her to know, as long as I don't get fired or something, how I feel about her, but if I don't, I don't. If I act poorly that's only a poor act and I'm never a rotten person because I don't *have to* act well, no matter how desirable it is. Then you'll get rid of downing yourself for your lack of expression of your feelings and then you'll get back and be able to assert yourself and I think even [*pounds for emphasis*] definitely, determinedly rather than angrily. When you're not angry at yourself, you'll be able to show her that she's not doing the right thing, that she's not a total louse for not doing the right thing. Do you see what I mean?

Fiona: Yes absolutely…

Ellis: Now if you would practise that; first just see that you down yourself, your father, her, nobody can down you, you do it by damning yourself, by needing love and needing to do the right thing. Secondly, seeing that when you're angry you damn others, you put them down rather than their behaviour and then thirdly, seeing that when you are not expressing your feelings, you go right back again to damning yourself. Now do you see that you're the one that is creating your self-downing and that you never have to, you can change that philosophy, then you could really change this. And then you could actively do it by doing our shame-attacking exercises or other risks – to speak up would be one of the main things, because you feel ashamed at times of speaking up. What's shameful about expressing your feelings even if people don't like you? Why is that shameful?

Fiona: Well, I've never looked at it as shameful. I've looked at it as…my opinions weren't that…um how can I put this. [*Ellis*: They weren't worthwhile?] Yeah, lack of confidence in my own conviction.

Ellis: But that's another word for shame. If I expressed myself, my feelings and my opinions aren't good enough and that's terrible, that's bad, that's shameful. You see that's just another form of shame.

Fiona: So shame…it takes the place of a lot of other expressions and feelings.

Ellis: That's right, self-downing, feelings of inadequacy, self-hatred, lack of confidence, they're all: 'I must do well and be loved and isn't it terrible and I'm no good if I'm not.' Now if you could see that and think against it and act against it, then you would be doing a very good thing and that's the homework I'd give you. To see that you're creating especially your shame, that you can change the philosophy that creates it and then you can act shamelessly, but don't get into trouble just act that way and take risks and see that you never have to down yourself for anything. Now do you think you could work on that?

Fiona: I know I could work on it…

Ellis: And it will take a while…

Fiona: That's the point, it's not going to be a revelation, I know that…

Ellis: Right, it's simple, but it's not easy and it takes a while. Now if you do that then I think you'll *feel* much better and then be able to take the new philosophy of 'I always accept myself no matter what' into other situations. So we're just using this as an illustration… OK it was very nice talking to you and you just go and think about that and work on that.

Fiona: I shall. Thank you.

3

Commentary on Ellis's Interview with Fiona

Ellis: Fiona, what problem would you mainly like to talk about today?

Rational Emotive Behaviour Therapy is a problem-focused and problem-solving approach to psychotherapy, and in his demonstration sessions Ellis implements the focus on client problems at the outset.

Fiona: Actually I would like to just express my feelings about myself and what is going on in my life that I can't seem to cope with.

Fiona responds by indicating that she wishes to *express her feelings* in a general sort of way. REBT therapists are not content just to help their clients express their feelings. They want to help their clients address and solve their emotional problems in a focused way.

Ellis: Yeah sure, especially what you can't seem to cope with then I'll see if we can give you some ideas on how to cope with what you presumably can't cope with.

Notice how Ellis focuses Fiona on her problems using her own words – 'especially what you can't seem to cope with' – and then introduces REBT's problem-solving emphasis by stating that he will give her some ideas 'on how to cope with what you presumably can't cope with'. This also engenders hope in the client.

Fiona: That would be terrific. Um...basically I would say my whole life has been a roller-coaster but it's much heavier at this point in my life...my feelings of anger towards the world and with that anger also goes a feeling of self-pity and despair. It kind of changes from that, in other words I don't want to feel angry and I don't know how to express my anger so I hold it inside of me and I take it and turn it around and hurt myself.

Fiona responds typically with Fa fairly general account of her problems which contains the following elements:

- a general sense of anger towards the world and not wanting to feel anger
- self-pity and despair
- non-expression of anger
- a vague statement of hurting herself with her anger

Ellis's immediate task is to help Fiona clarify her problems so that they can focus on something more specific. This is especially important in a one-off demonstration session.

Ellis: Yeah, well let me just see if I understand that. [*Fiona*: OK] I think you are saying that you have two feelings – one is that you feel very angry and you don't like that feeling, you don't want to feel that way but then you are also saying you feel like expressing the anger and you believe that if you express it, you will get it out and then it will go, but, since you don't express it, you then may put yourself down for not expressing it – is that correct?

In his attempt to understand Fiona from her frame of reference, Ellis focuses on:

- her anger and her wish to change this
- her non-expression of her anger and
- her depreciating herself for not expressing her anger

The latter is a meta-emotional problem (i.e. a second problem – self-depreciation – about an original problem – not expressing her anger) and is Ellis's attempt to make sense of Fiona's statement about turning her anger round and hurting herself with it.

In REBT, we distinguish between healthy anger (sometimes referred to as annoyance) and unhealthy anger. Ellis does not make any attempt to distinguish between these different types of anger. He considers Fiona's anger to be unhealthy and as you will see proceeds on that basis. In my assessment, I would have made an attempt to assess Fiona's anger more formally and ensure that it was unhealthy before proceeding. I would have done this by assessing how Fiona acted or felt like acting when she was angry and how she thought subsequent to making herself angry.

Fiona: Yes, so I'm angry at myself for not expressing it but I am also terrified of feeling and showing that anger because I don't know if I can control it. [*Ellis*: Right] Anger frightens me. It's been part of my life…I can't even handle yelling, it's just terrifying, it's hurt my whole life, it's hurt my marriages, my relationships with friends and family and…I would like to have a healthy attitude in terms of my feelings with anger because I end up hurting myself all the time. [*Ellis*: Right] It doesn't accomplish anything in my life [*Ellis*: Right] and it also reflects itself in my professional life. I can't seem to stay in one career and work where I can...at my age, I'm 36, I want to feel successful, I want to have a successful life...and really...

Fiona indicates that while she does depreciate herself for not express- ing her anger, she is afraid of it because she may not be able to control it and because of the negative effects that it has had on her life. The fact that she amplifies this point is indicative of it being more problematic for her.

Ellis: But as I see it, and again you correct me if I'm wrong, you have two levels: first the anger, which you are afraid might be really terrific and outstanding and overwhelm you, but then you are ter- rified about the anger [*Fiona*: Absolutely] because it knocks you off – is that right? [*Fiona*: ...Mm hmm] Why don't we start with the second one then we'll get back to the anger itself, but let's just talk about it first, if you want to, the terror about the anger. Do you want to start there and then we'll get back to the anger itself?

In this response, Ellis distinguishes between Fiona's primary problem – her anger – and her meta-emotional problem about her anger. Actually this latter problem is twofold: (a) Fiona's anxiety about losing control of her anger and (b) her fear of its effects on her life. Ellis does not distin- guish between the two. He notes that Fiona is terrified of her anger because 'it knocks you off', but this is a little vague and Ellis could have been clearer here.

Note that Ellis suggests that they begin with Fiona's meta-emotional problem (her problem about her anger) rather than her primary problem (her anger) without giving Fiona a rationale for doing so. He can get away with this because of his authority as an expert, but it is better practice to provide clients with a rationale for beginning with a meta-emotional problem and *then* ask for their agreement.

Fiona: The terror, since I've never been angry in my life I can only assume what I am going to feel and that is out of control.

Again Fiona indicates that her meta-emotional problem is anxiety about losing control should she be angry.

Ellis: Well, let's just assume the worst there, that you did, that you let yourself go on one occasion or a few occasions and you felt out of control, let's just suppose that, you got beyond yourself and you felt out of control. Now what are you afraid would happen then? Can you picture that out of controlledness and...?

This is an important intervention. Fiona has just said that she has never been angry in her life and that if she let herself be angry, then she infers that she will feel out control. Note that Ellis doesn't question this inference. Rather, he encourages her to assume the worst – that she lets herself experience anger and she does feel out of control – and then asks her what she would be afraid of then. What Ellis is doing here is using a technique known as inference chaining to discover what she is most anxious about. Note also that Ellis is encouraging Fiona to use imagery here.

Fiona: Yeah, I see myself shaking, I see myself…quivering. I see myself possibly killing – I don't know, it gets…I can't go that far with it [*Ellis*: Right] and I also see someone not liking me.

Note that Fiona comes up with three inferences here:

- shaking and quivering
- killing
- being observed by someone and that person not liking her

The second inference is clear evidence that her anger is unhealthy!

Ellis: Right. All right then let's just picture yourself shaking and quivering and feeling really murderous and somebody watching you or several people watching you and not liking you. Now, why would that be horrible if that were so, because we're deliberately now assuming the worst so to get you to see that even if you did express this anger it might not be the end of the world, but why would that be horrible if you expressed it, you got out of control *and* somebody or several people really disliked you?

In this response, Ellis does two things that I would not encourage novice REBT therapists to emulate. First, he assumes that Fiona believes that it is horrible to shake with anger, to feel murderous and to be disliked for getting out of control without checking this out with her. On theoretical grounds, Ellis is correct, of course, but if the client does not understand that she holds this awfulising belief or cannot see the relationship between this belief and her feelings of terror then she may resist any later interventions that are based on these points. Second, Ellis disputes Fiona's awfulising belief without helping her to understand what he is doing. Again, this may engender resistance if the client is confused about the therapist's line of questioning. Ellis would deal with such resistance if it becomes manifest and would thus do less than other REBT therapists to prepare the client for his interventions. I, for example, would have:

- checked that Fiona did hold an awfulising belief in this scenario;
- helped her to see the connection between this belief and her terror (the iB–C connection); and
- ensured that she understood why I was going to question her belief before doing so

Also, Ellis makes no attempt to identify which of Fiona's three inferences she is most anxious about.

Fiona: I really wouldn't know how to handle it, I wouldn't know how to…I can't handle people not liking me, it's…

In reply to Ellis's dispute, Fiona reveals that she is perhaps most anxious about people not liking her. Note that she did not answer Ellis's disputing question. This tells me that she wasn't prepared for therapeutic work directed at disputing her irrational beliefs at this point of the interview.

Ellis: Because you feel *what*? When people don't like you, what's your own feeling? Let's suppose people don't like you and that's specially because you are really out of control, you're angry, then how do you feel…?

Ellis now works with this inference, encourages Fiona to assume that people don't like her especially when out of control with anxiety and asks what her feeling about this would be.

Fiona: Then I feel they'll see me for who I am.

Note that Fiona does not provide her feeling, but another inference.

Ellis: And now let's suppose now that…
Fiona: They're seeing a horrible person.

Fiona completes the inference which is in full 'Others will see me for who I am…a horrible person.' The statement, 'for who I am' also reveals that this is Fiona's belief about herself at B in the ABC framework.

Ellis: All right now you prove to me that you are a horrible person if you're out of control and if people don't like you, how does that make *you* a horrible person?

Again without any preparation, Ellis disputes Fiona's irrational belief: 'I am a horrible person if I am out of control and people do not like me'.

Fiona: It's hard to answer that, you know…that's the whole problem.

Fiona reveals her struggle with the question.

Ellis: I know, but if we can get you to see that you are *not* a horrible person – you are a person *who* is acting, we'll say badly, very angrily out of control and unloved in this instance, then we'll solve maybe the most important part of your whole problem. But just think about that, you're out of control and people are *hating* you for being out of control. They are thinking you're a twerp, you're no good and you're really an impossible person. Now how does that make *you* no good?

This is a very typical Ellis intervention. He explains why Fiona isn't a horrible person and in doing so reveals to her the problem with the part–whole error – that one cannot legitimately rate one's whole self on the basis of a part of oneself – and tells her that if she really believes that she isn't a horrible person then she will solve what is perhaps the major part of her problem. Ellis provides Fiona with a clear motivation for the disputing that follows.

Fiona: Well actually it doesn't, it probably is the reverse, it would be good for me to be that way because it's healthy.

Fiona's response is confusing. She begins by seeming to understand that she isn't a horrible person for expressing her anger in an out of control way and then makes a fundamental shift and asserts that it would be good and healthy for her to express her anger in this way.

Ellis: Well, you're thinking that's healthy, that doesn't have to be…
Fiona: Healthy, meaning I can't be a smiling, lovely person all the time.
Ellis: That's right. I don't think personally from our standpoint in Rational Emotive Behaviour Therapy that it's really healthy to be angry, but it's healthy to be assertive, to be yourself [*Fiona*: That's it exactly] and if you were yourself and … [*Fiona*: I'd feel damned good] Right, but now let's suppose you're not just assertive, you're horribly angry. [*Fiona*: I'm horribly angry] You're getting upset about it. Now again why would you have to put *you* down – not the out of control down because that wouldn't be so good. Now why would you have to put you as a human down if that were so?

Ellis is very clear here in addressing Fiona's confusion in this response. He first briefly differentiates between healthy assertive anger and unhealthy anger and then encourages Fiona to assume that she is unhealthily angry. Having established the A clearly in Fiona's mind he

resumes his disputing intervention. The last few interchanges show that while disputing their clients' irrational beliefs, REBT therapists have to deal with a number of client misconceptions, misunderstandings and changes of tack along the way.

Fiona: Because it would reinforce what I think of myself.

Fiona reveals that her self-depreciation about this issue would reinforce a more general negative view of herself.

Ellis: And why do you think so badly of yourself?

Ellis picks up this more general theme. He does so because he can go from the specific level of communication to the general level and back again in a way that brings clarity to both levels for the client and makes the appropriate connections for the client between these levels. This is a skill that is well beyond less experienced REBT therapists.

Fiona: That goes back too long – it's too deep…it's too deeply embedded in me.
Ellis: Well I don't happen to think so. In Rational Emotive Behaviour Therapy we say that it does go back and you probably felt this way right from the beginning from age two, three or four because even then you had a certain implicit philosophy which you brought to any situation [*Fiona*: Correct] and that philosophy, do you know what that probably was, even at two, three, four and five?

Ellis teaches Fiona the important REBT theoretical principle that people bring an implicit self-depreciation philosophy to early and later experiences. This is typical of Ellis's work. He does not hesitate to teach key elements of REBT theory when he thinks this can be helpful to the client.

Fiona: I was a brat. [*Ellis*: Right] I provoked my father who *was* an angry person [*Ellis*: Right] and only because I wanted him to show me his love [*Ellis*: Right] but instead I didn't know how to handle him, I didn't understand what was going on, I would provoke him to get his attention and he would hit me.

Fiona doesn't answer Ellis's question, probably because she doesn't understand it. Instead, she provides some salient aspects of her early relationship with her father.

Ellis: All right, but you see you first provoked him to show his love. Now your philosophy behind that in regard to your being loved, what do you think that might have been?

Ellis brings Fiona back to the idea that her provoking behaviour was based on a philosophy.

Fiona: My philosophy then was to get his love, his attention [*Ellis*: Right] but it never worked that way.

Ellis: But was it just a desire or was it a *need*?

Fiona: It was a need [*Ellis* (*exaggerates*): Ahhh!] an absolute need.

Ellis helps Fiona to distinguish clearly between a desire for her father's love and her absolute need for it – a very common Ellis intervention.

Ellis: And that's what you brought to the situation at two, three, four, five, six. You had a dire *need*, necessity, for love and then you did anything – even acted brattily, did anything even against this father who was very angry himself. So your first philosophy that I see was a dire need for love, which incidentally I see you still having [*Fiona*: Absolutely] and that's why you did that.

But then there was a second philosophy which was probably there too; along with the dire need for love, and I'm just going to take a guess about it now – and you check me – that I *have* to act well, I *have* to do the right thing AND therefore be approved – is that possible, that you've always had that kind of philosophy?

REBT therapists do not generally write about developing an REBT case formulation with their clients, but this is exactly what Ellis is doing here. He is putting forward his understanding of some of Fiona's core irrational beliefs and outlining to her, based on the information she has given him, the effect that these beliefs have had on her behaviour. While her core irrational belief about needing love is clear, Ellis's hypothesis about Fiona having to act well and having to do the right thing and therefore be approved is more speculative.

Fiona: Yeah I had to be the nice sweet little Fiona. [*Ellis*: Right] People would like me and think what a nice little girl.

Ellis: But do you see the contradiction right from the start?

Fiona: I was rebelling against…

Ellis: That's a little later, first I have to be myself and win love, and almost every child wants to win love and be approved especially by her father, mother and people like that, but instead of I'd like to, I *have* to. And then when I'm not loved I'll do almost anything because I *have* to do well and *have* to be loved and I'll even rebel. I need: (1) the attention, love – but (2) I need to express myself even when it gets me into trouble – isn't that what you felt as a child? – and don't you still feel a lot of that conflict that…

Ellis's speculations here are based not so much on what Fiona has said in this interview as on his vast clinical experience of dealing with

clients with a similar story. Again, less experienced REBT therapists should stick much closer to the data provided by the client.

Also note that the words *underlined* here and elsewhere are indicative of the emphasis Ellis places on these words in the interview.

Fiona: Absolutely. I mean I did the same provocation in my marriage [*Ellis:* Yeah?] because I could not believe that this man could really love me and I had to test him all the time until he…er…he couldn't take it any longer.

Fiona seems to agree with Ellis's formulation, but actually focuses on her testing behaviour rather than on any need to express herself regardless of the trouble this gets her into. My own approach would be to actively involve the client more in disconfirming any of my hypotheses that may be faulty.

Ellis: So we're right back to I need, I absolutely must have his love and then I will even go to extremes and test people [*Fiona:* It's very frightening] and then when they fail the test and don't love you that much, how do you feel about them?

Ellis is now bringing to his developing formulation Fiona's anger that she mentioned at the beginning of the interview.

Fiona: Exactly; how do I feel about them?
Ellis: When you've tested your husband's love or your father's love and they failed and they didn't really love you as much as you thought they should…
Fiona: Then it actually…what it was doing was reinforcing the fact that I'm not a good person.

Fiona does not pick up the 'anger at others' theme.

Ellis: Ah reinforcing in your philosophy [*Fiona:* Yes] 'cos I *must* be loved and I *must* do well.
[*Ellis raps his fist against his hand to emphasise the word 'must'.*]

In this response, Ellis helps Fiona to see the relationship between her demands and her self-depreciation belief.

Fiona: He promised he would love me for ever, my father supposedly should have loved me no matter what and he didn't.
Ellis: Because he's my father?
Fiona: Because he's my father.
Ellis: Right, and my husband because he's my husband?
Fiona: Yes – and because he promised me that he'd love me for ever, but he didn't.

Ellis: And therefore what did that make him and them who promised to love you for ever and don't go through with it? What do you think about them…temporarily…when you need this love?

Fiona: I didn't think of them, I just thought of me in terms of they're right, I'm a terrible person.

Once again Fiona resists admitting condemning thoughts about these significant others. This could be in line with her self-imposed embargo on feeling angry towards others or she may not have such thoughts. It could also be due to the fact that Ellis isn't asking the right questions.

Ellis: That's one thing [*Fiona*: I put it all on me] but now let's get to the anger, did you also at times, not all the time, hate *them* for not giving you the love that you thought you needed?

Ellis tries again and this time mentions anger and hate. This seems to make the difference and indicates that he wasn't asking the right questions before.

Fiona: Of course I did.

Ellis: Ah – you see now that's two things. We start with *I* need the love, *I* should do the right thing and isn't it terrible, I'm an awful person when I don't, but then they should *see* my neediness and they should give in to it and they're terrible people. And then finally, or maybe not even finally, you add to that now I see I'm angry at the people I love and they love me less and isn't it horrible to be out of control and so brattish and so angry and you go right back to putting yourself down – isn't that right? [*Fiona*: Correct] Right.

Now let's unravel a couple of these things and show you what to do because I think it's very complicated – actually we've done it very, very briefly so you think a lot more about this – but I think it starts with a need to do well and be loved yourself. Then you get upset, self-downing, then you get angry at them for not giving it, then you get angry at you for being angry at them and maybe losing control, being brattish. But let's just take one of these things again, get back to that – the fundamental need to be loved, to do well with others. Now I'm not going to by any means debate or dispute your desire because everybody desires love. It's one of the most fine, the greatest things in the world, it really makes for relating, but you from the start and right now *have* to be loved and you *need* to be loved and you're viewing yourself as a terrible person when you're not. Now why *must* you be loved, not why do you desire it, why do you *have* to be…?

Ellis provides an REBT-based formulation of Fiona's problems as a succinct summary. Then he states the importance of dealing with a few

elements of this complexity in a problem-solving way. Otherwise Fiona will only gain insight into the REBT-based formulation of her problems.

Fiona: It's an interesting point um…throughout my life it's always been, life was, I never was myself in terms of…I never knew who I was because I was always going by the standards of what their expectations for me were.

Ellis: Right or what you thought their expectations were.

Fiona: Or what I thought their expectations were [*Ellis*: Right] and primarily it seemed that I…er…I had to be married you know [*Ellis*: Right] in a very secure situation…so that's how I based my life…not in terms of what was expected of me.

Ellis: Right. To be a good person I had to fulfil what *they* expected of me.

Once again Ellis goes with Fiona's reflections on living up to people's expectations and quickly shows Fiona her relevant irrational belief.

Fiona: So I've never really done anything for me. I really never found out what I really need.

Ellis: Well, how can you when you're fundamentally…

Fiona: I couldn't and at this time of my life I'm trying to. So what I've done is eliminated love completely from my life, in fact people. I'm totally alone now.

Fiona shows how she has solved the problems of needing to live up to the actual or presumed expectations of others – she has eliminated people from her life!

Ellis: But that throws out the baby with the bathwater. Now suppose we could get you to see that you don't *need* love, it's very desirable, but you don't *need* it and you don't *have to* conform to what other people say you *should* conform to, though it would be nice if they did care for you, and then you would be able to risk getting involved if you really got rid of that *dire* necessity for doing the right thing and being loved. Now how could that be done? How could any human, you included, get rid of not the desire, we're not trying to get rid of that, 'cos you've really thrown out the baby with the bathwater, the desire. [*Fiona*: At this point, yes] How can you keep the desire to be loved, to be approved, to get along with others, to relate and *not* the necessity, the dire need that puts you down. How could you do that?

Ellis quickly shows Fiona that her decision to eliminate other people is flawed and is still based on the idea that she needs to be loved and that she needs to conform. He once again distinguishes between her desires

and needs and asks her how she can retain the former and get rid of the latter.

Fiona: Well, I think becoming my own person, number one.

Fiona gives a vague answer, a useful one, but vague nevertheless.

Ellis: That would be one. That's excellent because then you see you'd risk being *you* and your philosophy would be 'I'm going to be me at all costs' and [*Fiona*: Right] and *if* they don't love me what could you conclude? They don't love me when I'm me. What could you conclude about that?

Ellis reinforces Fiona's response and then provides part of the healthy philosophy behind her response: 'I'm going to be me at all costs' (the 'at all costs' is rigid, however). Note that Ellis then asks Fiona to think about the second part of her implicit rational philosophy. This is something that Ellis does a lot in his demonstration sessions: making a point didactically, but then encouraging the client to think for herself about some aspect of that point. In this way, he shares the workload with the client.

Fiona: Well, it's not that I'm a bad person though [*Ellis*: Right] because I'm happy with me [*Ellis*: Right] which is something I'm trying to work on.

Fiona's response is along the right lines, but put somewhat tentatively.

Ellis: Right. You could conclude: 'Maybe it's too bad, I would wish they would like me as me and there must be somebody in the universe who would like me as me, you see, but they don't *have* to' – it's the necessity, [*pounds for emphasis*] the *demand* that does it not the desire. Now if you could really work on that 'I'd like to be me' primarily and then secondarily get those people to care for me who will accept me as ME. Wouldn't that solve a great deal of the problem?

Ellis is making two points here. First, he once again shows Fiona the difference between a preference for being liked and a demand to be. He has done this several times already and she hasn't quite got the point. REBT therapists often have to make the same point several times before clients understand. Ellis repeats these points without a hint of impatience. Second, he urges Fiona to seek out people who will accept her for herself. I might have stressed the importance of doing the former before the latter, otherwise Fiona might avoid people who conditionally accept her because of her need to be liked.

Fiona: Yes, because I think at that point – if it should ever happen again – um…it would be a healthy relationship [*Ellis*: Right] it would not be that neurotic need and that provocation and that anger.

Ellis: And you've already implied from what you said a couple of minutes ago – the active solution, because if you would change your philosophy to 'I'm primarily going to be me and if they like me, great, but if they don't like me I can still accept myself as me', that would be fine if you thought that way, but one way to think that way is what you said 'to take risks' and what you might try are some of our shame-attacking exercises. Do you know anything about those?

Ellis stresses the importance of acting in ways that are consistent with developing rational beliefs. Because Fiona has a need to be liked, he introduces the idea of her undertaking one or more shame-attacking exercises. These are designed to give clients an opportunity to practise the philosophy of unconditional self-acceptance in the face of disapproval from others for acting 'shamefully'.

Fiona: No, I've no idea.

Ellis: Well, you think of something that you consider shameful to do in public, in front of people, now not to hurt anybody, we don't want you to slap anybody in the face or get arrested – walk naked, you could walk naked in a public square and that would be shameful – but something like not tipping a waiter or taxi-cab driver [*Fiona (laughs)*: Oh I do that] Well, that's not it then…or buy an outlandish costume dress and then never wearing it because you're ashamed to. [*Fiona*: Because of the shame] Yeah, you need something that you consider shameful. We get people to do foolish things, we get them to go on the New York subway, for example, and yell out the stops '42nd STREET' at the top of their lungs and to stay on the train you see. Or to go to Macy's or Bloomingdale's and yell out the time '11.50 AND A THIRD' and to stand there with everybody looking at them. Or to take a banana and a long leash and to walk the banana and take another banana and feed the first banana – to do foolish things. In public you can go right out on the street and stop somebody and say 'I just got out of the loony-bin what day is it?'

Fiona: Well, what purpose will that serve? [*Ellis*: The purpose is that you can pick something] – that this is what I'm doing and I don't care about the rest of the world?

The above exchanges show that Fiona does not see the value of doing such exercises in helping her overcome her particular problems.

Ellis: Well, to pick something that *you* consider shameful. Not that I do and to do it in public that's the first part, not get arrested, not get in trouble and then as you do it in public to work on not feeling ashamed, because shame is the essence of self-downing, of self-hatred. You see and if you can do these things in public and really not feel ashamed because *you* know why you're doing them, you know you're doing them for you, you know in this case they're even therapeutic, then that kind of thing helps you to resist the pressure which people have put on you since early childhood – and always will – and stops you from downing yourself.

Fiona: But why does it have to be something so absurd?

Ellis: Well, it doesn't. I'm just saying…actually it would be better if you pick something that you are normally ashamed to do and would be helpful for you…

Fiona: Yeah…like…like getting angry.

Ellis: That's right you could do that…

Fiona: Like screaming at someone.

It is interesting that it is Fiona rather than Ellis who suggests an exercise linked directly to her problem in expressing anger.

Ellis: That's right, you could deliberately scream. You'd pick somebody that's not too vulnerable – because we don't want you to hurt them – we don't want you to pick a little child or something like that, but somebody that you could get temporarily angry towards – scream at them, because you feel ashamed, not feel ashamed and then later show them why you did it, you see because we don't want anybody else to be hurt in the process. Or something else where you would really be thoroughly ashamed to do it, to risk it because all your life you have avoided this risk, you've sat on your feelings, you've sat on your anger, you've sat on everything and avoided it. Now if we can get you to do it and not put yourself down, not feel ashamed, that would be a long way towards solving your problems. You see. Then you could look at your anger, when you feel angry inside and you feel enraged with people and also acknowledge that you're creating the anger, do you know why you are creating the anger?

Ellis outlines a number of cautions concerning Fiona deliberately screaming at people in order to accept herself for her actions and for being disapproved for doing so. There is evidence in what he says that he is not keen for her to do that since he suggests that she does something else. When suggesting shame-attacking exercises to clients it is important to consider their likely impact on others. As Ellis says to Fiona, 'we don't want anybody else to be hurt in the process'.

Note that when Ellis changes the topic at the end of his response, Fiona doesn't understand the point he is making. Since REBT is a psycho-educational approach to therapy, its practitioners impart a lot of information during the course of therapy. The purpose of REBT education is client learning, so REBT therapists need to give a lot of thought to how much information they impart and how they do this. Monitoring signs of client confusion and lack of understanding is a key therapist task in REBT.

Fiona: Can you repeat that last...?

Ellis: When, let's suppose, ...give me an instance recently where you got angry at somebody, you got very angry...you just felt it, not that you expressed it.

Ellis is now going to help Fiona understand the cognitive dynamics of her anger. Note that he asks Fiona for a specific example of her anger. This is a common tactic in the early phase of REBT.

Fiona: I don't express it. Um...Someone I work with...she...er...everything goes right for her...she gets all the great accounts, she gets dates, she gets roses sent to her every day, and I sit there and my stomach is in knots and I feel like saying – and then she complains...'Oh'...'Ooh'...You know she's just a spoilt person who has no true values, she's not sensitive and caring and she...everything good happens to her and I hate her. [*Ellis*: All right] and I get very angry because she hurt me as well.

Ellis: Right...so at (A) an Activating Event in the ABCs of REBT, she acts this way and let's suppose she's doing you in and she's acting badly, and she's a spoilt brat herself. Let's assume that. [*Fiona*: This is her] Exactly. And at (C) a Consequence in your gut, you're feeling enraged, you're not doing anything about it. No...but you're feeling enraged. Now in Rational Emotive Behaviour Therapy we think that you're making yourself enraged. She is not enraging you...

For the first time in this interview, Ellis introduces REBT's famous ABC model and makes the key point that Fiona makes herself feel angry about her work colleague. Her work colleague does not make her angry.

Fiona: You are right about that. [*Ellis*: Right, so what are you doing?] No one else is being annoyed by her.

Ellis: That's exactly the point. [*Fiona*: Only I] Right so at (B), your Belief System, you are telling yourself something about her that is making you angry and I could guess from our theory, our ABC theory, what it is – but let's see if you could figure it out. What are you saying whenever you are angry at her?

Note that Ellis makes a general point didactically and then encourages Fiona to apply this to her situation. If she understands the point that

Ellis is endeavouring to make, she will reply that she is demanding that her work colleague must not act in the way that she acts.

Fiona: Oh I know what I'm saying. [*Ellis*: What?] She doesn't deserve it, why her? [*Ellis*: Why her?] Why her? I'm working so much harder and I have had so many more problems in my life, why is everything good happening to her [*Ellis*: As?] she doesn't deserve it…

Fiona's reply is typical of clients in the early phase of REBT. She puts her thoughts in the form of rhetorical questions (e.g. 'why her?). These are often indirect expressions of irrational beliefs.

Ellis: Right and she *shouldn't* be getting away with this. That's what I hear. [*Fiona*: Right] All right, now we ask in REBT – we go to (D), Disputing: Why *shouldn't* [*pounds for emphasis*] she act that way and get away with it? Why must she act well?

Ellis makes explicit Fiona's irrational belief. Fiona confirms her agreement and Ellis proceeds to dispute this belief. Note that apart from informing Fiona that he is going to D (Disputing) in the now expanded ABCD framework, Ellis once again does not prepare her for his disputing interventions. Ellis's line of questioning shows that he is empirically disputing Fiona's irrational beliefs. Empirical disputes basically ask whether clients' demands are true are false. They are, of course, false (see Chapter 1).

REBT theory distinguishes among several different meanings of the word 'should'. Only the absolute should is regarded as irrational and this a target for change (Dryden, 1998b). As such my own practice is to use the qualifier 'absolute' when discussing and disputing irrational shoulds with clients. I do this to be clear that I am only targeting absolute shoulds for change, as noted above. Ellis does not do this here, nor is it his practice to do so more generally.

Fiona: There is no why, there is no reason why she should do anything.

Fiona gives the correct answer to Ellis's disputing question.

Ellis: That's right. Now if you really believe that, you believe it at this second, then you would be sorry and displeased and annoyed at her behaviour, but you wouldn't be upset and angry at her. If you really believe she *should* act the way she does because she does…

Ellis notes that Fiona has provided the correct answer but doesn't really believe it yet. He then shows that if she did really believe it she would experience healthier negative emotions at C in the ABC framework.

This encourages Fiona to work on changing her beliefs because there is a good reason to do so. This is known as pragmatic disputing of irrational beliefs.

Fiona: Not that she should, I mean this is a person, her own personality, and her own whatever...um...I can't have her feel or think the way I do [*Ellis*: Right] but it does upset me to think she's intelligent enough that she should be able to see it and she doesn't...

Fiona's response here is interesting. She *seems* to acknowledge that her work colleague does not have to be the way she wants her to, but in the next moment she reveals her demand that because her work colleague is intelligent enough she should (in the absolute sense of the word) be able to see a particular point. Clients often can see that in general people don't have to be the way they want them to be, but go back to demanding that they do so in specific situations. This shows the importance of helping clients to dispute their irrational beliefs both generally and specifically (see DiGiuseppe, 1991b).

Ellis: But I say she shouldn't be able to see it. [*Fiona*: I understand that] Do you know why she shouldn't be able – even though she's intelligent – why should she act the way she does? Do you know why she should?

Ellis is being confusing here, a rare instance when he is not being clear. One of Ellis's hallmarks as an REBT therapist, both in demonstration sessions and in his regular therapy sessions, is the clarity of his communications.

Fiona: She shouldn't...

Fiona shows her confusion.

Ellis: No, she should.
Fiona: Oh why she should act the way she is...[*Ellis*: Badly]...because this is her.

After a very brief period of confusion, Ellis and Fiona are back on track and again Fiona reveals her intellectual understanding of the rational alternative to her irrational belief (see Chapter 1.)

Ellis: That's her nature...Right. [*Fiona*: That's right] Now whenever we're angry we're denying the nature of others. Now I'm not saying it's good that she acts that way, I'm assuming with you, it's bad, obnoxious, annoying that she should act annoyingly if that's her nature to act annoyingly.

Ellis makes two points here. He emphasises Fiona's rational belief and shows Fiona that he isn't challenging her inference at A that her colleague is acting badly. When you challenge clients' anger-creating irrational beliefs at B they often think that you are challenging their inferences at A. Making clear that you are not doing so is an important part of the disputing process, as Ellis shows.

Fiona: Just as I should get angry if that's how I feel...

Fiona applies the point about shoulds to her own beliefs about her feelings of anger. It is encouraging when clients do this spontaneously since it shows that they are actively processing the content of the session and looking for ways of applying what they learn to aspects of their problems not currently under discussion.

Ellis: That's exactly right. Now it's not good that she acts that way nor even that you get angry. You'd better be *assertive* [*pounds for emphasis*] without anger, because anger is a damnation of her, you're damning her for her act, and if you're wise you'll say: 'Damnit I don't like what she is doing, I wish she wouldn't, and I'll probably tell her one of these days about it and try to get her to change.'

Some clients think that empirically correct statements such as 'She should act badly' or 'I should be angry' condone bad behaviour. Ellis indicates that this is not the case even though Fiona has not indicated that she believed it was. He then shows her again that the healthy behavioural alternative to her anger is assertion and links this to the rational belief that underpins assertion while contrasting it with the other depreciation that is a feature of anger.

Fiona: Oh I would love to, that would be a very good step in the right direction.

Fiona clearly shows that she wants to be assertive.

Ellis: Right, but if we got you un-angry but still displeased with her behaviour and then assertive and we got you to not down yourself in case she and other people came back [*pounds for emphasis*] at you when you're assertive, wouldn't that solve the problem?

Notice how comprehensive and concise Ellis is here in this short statement. He is showing Fiona that she can:

- make herself displeased rather than angry about her work colleague's behaviour;
- assert herself with her colleague;
- accept herself in the face of her colleague's (and others') negative reaction to her assertion.

He then shows her that if she is able to do these three things then she will solve her problem. Such statements show clients what is possible and often serve to encourage clients to do the difficult work that is necessary to achieve their goals.

Fiona: It would certainly help.

Ellis: Right, then the thing to do, and you can do it in both orders, you can work on the anger first or the self-downing, the shame and determine that hereafter whenever things like this happen with people like her – and she's just an example, there are thousands of them – I will always think my thoughts and accept my thoughts and my feelings about her and even if she learns about my feelings, because I may tell her, and she puts me down I will accept myself no matter what she and other people think. [*Fiona*: I see] You see, I won't say I'm right, because I may be wrong, but even when I'm *wrong* I'll accept myself, because I am I and I have the right to be wrong. Now I'll try to be correct, but I don't *have* to be correct, I don't *have* to be approved by them you see…Then secondly – now that I'm ready to accept myself, I'll see that (1) I am displeased by her behaviour, but (2) I am damning her, I'm saying she *must* not do what she is indubitably doing and she *must* do it right now because that's the way she is right now, I wish she wouldn't and therefore I will assert myself and take the risk she won't love me, she won't like me at all, but she doesn't *have to* change, it is just highly desirable. D'you see?

Ellis has outlined in one large chunk all that Fiona needs to do to help herself with all the problems that she has brought up in the session. She may agree with him (and her response indicates that she does), but can she retain all this information? REBT is more about what the client takes away from sessions than about the amount of ground that client and therapist cover in sessions. In my view, Fiona is too passive at this point of the session.

Fiona: Absolutely.

Ellis: Now if we can get you to work along that line – on mainly your self-downing because I still think that's your biggest problem… and incidentally we'll go to one other thing and that is: let's suppose now that you're trying to work along the lines we're saying and you still run away, you still don't assert yourself and you don't go for yourself, and you run away and you avoid the situation, you cop out et cetera. Now again at (A), Activating Event, you're copping out, you're not expressing yourself, you're not being yourself. At (B), Belief System, you're telling yourself something which we'll get back to in a second and then at (C), you're feeling ashamed of your own copping out, because at (B) what are you saying again about *you* for copping out, for not expressing your feelings?

Ellis's goal is clearly to cover all aspects of Fiona's problems because after his comprehensive summary above he introduces the theme again of Fiona depreciating herself about her lack of assertion. I am reminded here of Ellis's comments on his famous session with Gloria in the first *Three approaches to psychotherapy* **film series (Shostrom, 1965). He said of his performance, which drew quite a bit of negative criticism, that he tried to do too much with Gloria in too short a time. The same criticism could be levelled at Ellis here at this point of the session. To offset this criticism, it could be said that if Fiona was given an audiotape for later review (see Chapter 1), even if she couldn't process everything during the session she could do so at her leisure later. However, it is not clear from the information that I have to hand about this interview that she was given a tape of the session.**

Fiona: I'm feeling angry…[*Ellis*: Right] I'm feeling the anger.
Ellis: Right, but what are you saying about not expressing feelings and copping out and running out of the situation and withdrawing? What are you saying about *you*, you know you're angry, you know you're non-assertive and you're not doing anything, now what are you telling yourself about your behaviour of copping out?
Fiona: At that point?
Ellis: Yeah, when you notice that you've copped out and not said anything.
Fiona: Well, let's see…I can't really verbalise it…

Fiona is still having difficulty identifying her irrational beliefs at this point.

Ellis: Well, you're not liking yourself are you? [*Fiona*: No, I know that]… so you're saying, I copped out…

An interesting response from Ellis. Rather than informing Fiona what she was telling herself to create her shame about not expressing her anger, he speculates on what she wasn't telling herself. He is giving the client some help, but is not doing all the work for her.

Fiona: I'm er…I'm that bad person again. [*Ellis*: That's right] I'm that stupid person, I'm that incompetent person, that child, whatever…

Ellis's response has helped Fiona to pinpoint her self-depreciation belief, but will she be able to do this for herself after the session?

Ellis: That's right. Now you see the vicious circle, you began with self-downing to begin with and that's probably why you didn't speak up. You made yourself very angry. Then you were non-assertive about your feelings and on both levels the original one to down yourself and not speak up and then you blame yourself for not speaking up, so you do a double whammy [*Fiona (laughs)*: It's a vicious circle, right] Right, you see. Now I say that if you start at the end again and say to yourself – 'Yes I didn't express myself, that was foolish because I would like her to know, as long as I don't get fired or something, how I feel about her, but if I don't, I don't. If I act poorly that's only a poor act and I'm never a rotten person because I don't *have to* act well, no matter how desirable it is. Then you'll get rid of downing yourself for your lack of expression of your feelings and then you'll get back and be able to assert yourself and I think even [*pounds for emphasis*] definitely, determinedly rather than angrily. When you're not angry at yourself, you'll be able to show her that she's not doing the right thing, that she's not a total louse for not doing the right thing. Do you see what I mean?

Rather than help her to dispute her self-depreciation belief, Ellis puts this problem into the broader mix of her problems. However, he does suggest an order to tackling her problems, which is helpful since clients with different problems or different components of the same problem are often at a loss as to where to start in helping themselves.

Fiona: Yes absolutely…
Ellis: Now if you would practise that; first just see that you down yourself, your father, her, nobody can down you, you do it by damning yourself, by needing love and needing to do the right thing. Secondly, seeing that when you're angry you damn others, you put them down rather than their behaviour and then thirdly, seeing that when you are not expressing your feelings, you go right back again to damning yourself. Now do you see that you're the one that is creating your self-downing and that you never have to, you can change that philosophy, then you could really change this. And then you could actively do it by doing our shame-attacking exercises or other risks – to speak up would be one of

the main things, because you feel ashamed at times of speaking up. What's shameful about expressing your feelings even if people don't like you? Why is that shameful?

Ellis gives Fiona yet another summary statement and then picks up a further theme to focus on. This time it is shame about expressing herself and being disliked.

Fiona: Well, I've never looked at it as shameful. I've looked at it as…my opinions weren't that…um how can I put this. [*Ellis*: They weren't worthwhile?] Yeah, lack of confidence in my own conviction.

Fiona doesn't resonate with shame.

Ellis: But that's another word for shame. If I expressed myself, my feelings and my opinions aren't good enough and that's terrible, that's bad, that's shameful. You see that's just another form of shame.

Ellis shows Fiona that she really does feel shame even if she has another phrase for it.

Fiona: So shame…it takes the place of a lot of other expressions and feelings.
Ellis: That's right, self-downing, feelings of inadequacy, self-hatred, lack of confidence, they're all: 'I must do well and be loved and isn't it terrible and I'm no good if I'm not.' Now if you could see that and think against it and act against it, then you would be doing a very good thing and that's the homework I'd give you. To see that you're creating especially your shame, that you can change the philosophy that creates it and then you can act shamelessly, but don't get into trouble just act that way and take risks and see that you never have to down yourself for anything. Now do you think you could work on that?

Ellis develops the theme of shame and unilaterally gives Fiona a homework assignment. The assignment is quite general and philosophical, rather than specific and practical. Although Fiona indicates below that she can work at this, readers will judge for themselves whether she was able to implement this assignment. I, for one, have my doubts.

Fiona: I know I could work on it…
Ellis: And it will take a while…
Fiona: That's the point, it's not going to be a revelation, I know that…
Ellis: Right, it's simple, but it's not easy and it takes a while. Now if you do that then I think you'll feel much better and then be able to

take the new philosophy of 'I always accept myself no matter what' into other situations. So we're just using this as an illustration…OK it was very nice talking to you and you just go and think about that and work on that.

Ellis makes two important points here: that developing self-acceptance takes time and while it may seem simple it is difficult to do in practice. Fiona is clearly impressed by what she is learning in the session, but will she be able to put what she learns into practice?

Fiona: I shall. Thank you.

Feedback

What follows is a brief interview carried out with Fiona after the session, designed to gauge her reactions to the session. I will add my comments at various points.

Interviewer: OK, Fiona, I want to ask you a little bit about your reactions to the session and to Dr Ellis. Did you feel that he was with you, that he really had a grasp of the things that you were disturbed about and the issues that were important to you?

Fiona: Absolutely…In fact he seemed to be ahead of me, as if he knew me without any information prior to our sitting here…He was ahead of me.

Fiona considers that Ellis was tuned in to her, but that he was ahead of her. Readers should ask themselves whether or not this is productive in the practice of REBT.

Interviewer: Yeah, in what ways in particular did you feel that he was really tuned in and he really hit the nail on the head?

Fiona: Well, he was able to…er …take the problem and open it up and let me see it and bring out things that I…as I said I hadn't mentioned to him, but was feeling all along and that helped me to understand that I'm not that unique in some respects that I'm not loony-bin bad, but I do have a problem that's not that terribly unique and he knows how to deal with it.

Fiona is revealing both specific and non-specific aspects of REBT. With respect to the specific aspects, she mentions Ellis's ability to focus on her problems and accurately assess them as well as inspiring in her the confidence that he knows how to deal with them. With respect to the non-specific aspects, she mentions the sense of universality she derived from the session – that she is not unique or 'loony-bin bad' for having her problems.

Interviewer: How were you feeling at the start of the session? What emotions were you experiencing?

Fiona: Anxiety…absolutely, but it started out very easily…and it became more comfortable every minute. I didn't realise that this was…you know…something that was being taped. It was between him and I…I didn't feel the world was looking.

Interviewer: Did you feel cut off at any point at all by him?

Fiona: No, he let me open up, he didn't stop me at any time.

Critics of REBT often complain that REBT therapists cut their clients off or stop them from exploring important aspects of their experience. Clearly, this was not Fiona's experience.

Interviewer: How are you feeling about some of the problems that you talked about?

Fiona: I see that there are ways of working with it where you don't have to go into therapy for eight or ten years to deal with some problems. You can…there is a method and I'd like to try it. Um…when I leave here.

Fiona has seen that REBT is a problem-solving approach to psychotherapy and one that can be used from the outset.

Interviewer: And was there any insight in particular or any idea in particular that you got out of the session that you're really going to work on trying to adopt or [use to] replace some of your previous ideas?

Fiona: Er…Well the feeling that the other person that I'm angry at should be that person because that is that person. I can't take it away from that person and expect the world to be the way I see it and by accepting that, I have the feeling my anger will diminish and I can handle it with a different approach.

Even though Ellis perhaps placed most emphasis on self-depreciation with Fiona, she most readily remembers the empirical point that others should be the way that they are. If she remembers this and applies it in her life then the session will have been very successful.

Interviewer: And how optimistic do you feel about being able to do that?

Fiona: Optimistic.

Interviewer: You do?

Fiona: Yeah.

Interviewer: OK. Is there anything else you would like to share with me about the session or the reactions that you had to it?

Fiona: I…it was absolutely beneficial…er…I came in feeling quite depressed and I can't wait to go outside and see the sun today.

Fiona clearly indicates the immediate benefits of the session.

Interviewer: That's great. OK, thank you very much.
Fiona: Thank you.

4

Ellis's Interview with Linda

Ellis: What problem would you like to start with?

Linda: Well, I have a problem when my partner talks about previous girl-friends. I feel that I should just ignore it because he is seeing me, but it, it bothers me…it makes me…it bothers me a lot…

Ellis: Well, how do you feel when he mentions these other women, which of course he doesn't have to, how do you feel?

Linda: Mad – [*Ellis*: Yeah so you're angry] real mad!

Ellis: Because you're telling yourself what, to make yourself angry at him?

Linda: Am I telling myself I do not like myself?

Ellis: No, no that would make you angry at you, but what are you say-ing about him to make you angry at him?

Linda: I feel that he should be concentrating on me. Why isn't he think-ing…why aren't you liking *me* why are you even thinking about anyone else?

Ellis: So you're observing that he is not concentrating on you, as far as you can see and then you are feeling very angry at him because he should be concentrating on you – isn't that right?

Linda: Yeah.

Ellis: And then when you are angry and you know you're angry, how do you feel about you being angry at him?

Linda: I don't know if I think about that, I kind of want to sulk, I'd like to withdraw and not talk to him or run away. If I thought about it I'd probably feel guilty, like I'm acting like a pain in the neck.

Ellis: Right but you don't think about that too much – when you're angry at him, you don't feel guilty?

Linda: Not while I'm with him.

Ellis: No OK but then let us suppose you go away and then you remem-ber you were angry.

Linda: I wouldn't like myself for it.

Ellis: Because, and let's start with that, you have two symptoms that most people have. First we'll call it anger, and we will get back to that in a few minutes. And then you feel guilty later when you remember that you were that angry about him and that out of control. Now let's just start with the secondary one the guilt first and let's suppose that you remember and feel guilty now that you felt angry. What are you saying to yourself about being angry that makes you feel guilty? So what do you think that is? What are you telling yourself to make you feel guilty about your anger?

Linda: Well, I should be nice, I should be pleasant when I'm with him and the wonderful person that I am, and instead I feel more like a bitch.

Ellis: 'I should be nice like all other women would be in this position.' Right but why *must* you be nice?

Linda: That he will not like me maybe if I am not?

Ellis: That's what would be desirable, and most people think in that way. Just because it's desirable to be nice, which let us assume that it is desirable, therefore I must...act desirably. Now does it follow that, even if it is very desirable for you not to be angry with him just to be nice, that you *have* to do what's desirable?

Linda: Well no, I guess I don't think about it I just go ahead and get mad.

Ellis: Well you jump, I say you do think about it, you jump from because it is desirable – I shouldn't have done that. At the moment you're focusing on your madness and we'll get back to that. But do you see that even if you went on for the rest of your life fool-ishly making yourself angry at people like him that that would be allowable? That you could still accept yourself without guilt, do you see that that is so?

Linda: By talking to myself a different way and saying that that is OK.

Ellis: Not it's OK, because anger isn't OK, you see that would probably ruin your relationships or interrupt your relationship with him, but I'm OK. I can accept me myself even when I act in a non-OK manner such as anger, you see?

Linda: All right, I would have to brainwash myself to think that. Let's see...I'm OK even when I get angry and don't like certain things. I don't see it that way, I feel I still see myself as, you know, kind of bitchy and not easygoing.

Ellis: That's OK if you want to see a characteristic or trait of yours as bitchy, but you are not a bitch even when you're bitchy. Do you see why you're still not a bitch even when you are bitchy? Do you see why that is?

Linda: I'm OK even though I'm bitchy?

Ellis: And you're not a bitch because a bitch would be completely, thoroughly bitchy all the time.

Linda: Oh, I see, I'm saying one little incident makes me...

Ellis: That's right and also a bitch would be damnable and not OK and so it has two meanings: (1) that I'm thoroughly this way – which is false, and (2) that I am thoroughly damnable because I am sometimes this way. You see your basic demand on yourself is that I *must not* be bitchy *at all* under any conditions. Now is that likely – that you are never going to be bitchy under any conditions?

Linda: No, but then maybe I am going to say to myself then 'OK. I can go ahead and be a bitch because you know I'm not a total bitch, I'm still a nice person.'

Ellis: Right, but why wouldn't you say that? Let's suppose we get you to accept you with your bitchiness. Now why wouldn't you say 'What difference would it make I'll just go ahead and be bitchy and knock them all off with my bitchiness,' why wouldn't you say that?

Linda: Well, because…I'd like to be a little bit easier going, it would make my life easier.

Ellis: That's right because it is *preferable* to be unbitchy not *necessary*, which you are saying it is, and I'm no good if I don't do what is necessary. But it's *preferable* to be unbitchy and even if you accepted you with your bitchiness you'd work against the bitchiness and try to be less bitchy and try to be less angry, which brings us back to the original problem. Now let us go back to the anger, once you accept yourself with your bitchiness, with your anger: it is still unpreferable, still undesirable and so you want to give it up – the anger. Now the anger, he, we'll assume, is doing what you said. You could of course be making all this up but I'll assume you are describing correctly and he is gratuitously, needlessly talking about these other women when he could shut his big mouth. Right?

Linda: Right.

Ellis: He doesn't have to talk about them. OK so what are you saying to you about him when you are angry about him opening his big mouth talking about these other women?

Linda: I don't like him when he is doing that.

Ellis: He's doing the wrong thing and I don't like him as a human. He *must not* do that wrong thing. Right? Well why must he not do the wrong thing even if it is wrong?

Linda: Well I thought about that, maybe I need to control the situation, I'm going to set the rules and that's not acceptable.

Ellis: OK so why must you control, it's good to control (probably), but why *must* you, why *need* you control him and the situation?

Linda: I bet we're getting back to I don't like myself if I cannot control the situation.

Ellis: Well partly that is it, if I didn't totally control the situation I would be a pretty rotten person so I think you do have that in there. But there is another reason why people have to control the world aside from self-downing, putting themselves down because of loss of control. Do you know why they demand perfect control?

Linda: No.

Ellis: Because they *have* to get exactly what they want when they want it.

Linda: They have to have get…oh.

Ellis: Therefore I *must* control him and make him say what I want him to say and only what I want him to say.

Linda: So this would go along with something else. If he does not demonstrate and tell me I like you, I really like you and I'm going to change my life tomorrow since I met you. This is the same things as controlling, as I have to have my way.

Ellis: I have to have my way and also if I don't I'm uncontrolling and a rotten person. You see there are two ideas there: (1) I need what I want, and if I want it I must have it. And then (2), if I am unable to arrange what I want there is something poor and weak about me and I cannot stand me.

Linda: All right now that first thing you said: if I cannot have what I want because I want it, is that like being a spoilt brat?

Ellis: Well it's like being a brat, I'm not sure you had to be spoilt. You see most children, young children are that way even if they are not spoilt.

Linda: So why aren't most adults like that or is it normal/ordinary?

Ellis: No, it is very common that adults refuse to give up the original childish philosophy and most children, practically all of them have this philosophy: 'Because I want it I should have it. You must give it to me, I should run the universe.' Now some of us decide that we don't run the universe and we don't have to even though it would be nice if we did – and we become mature. But most humans remain immature all their lives and have low frustration tolerance or what I call discomfort anxiety or anxiety about the discomfort of not getting what they want and they don't change their philosophy.

Linda: Oh, I like that.

Ellis: Now you're able to…

Linda: I never thought that was part of growing up that you realise you don't get what you want just because you want it.

Ellis: But isn't it part of growing up, just think of a couple of mature people that you might know – that's if you know any because most people are immature – now don't they, when they get disappointed, when they don't get what they want, don't they conclude something like 'Too bad. I don't need what I want'.

Linda: I don't care really.

Ellis: Well not I don't care at all, because they still would care but they would be very sorry that…

Linda: But that is what I have always said.

Ellis: Yeah but that is like the fox and the grapes. The fox cannot get the grapes so he says, 'Who needs the grapes?' But that is wrong. He had better say 'I, the fox, want the grapes and therefore I'll keep jumping or look for other grapes or eat a banana but I don't *need* what I want.' So he ends up with a rationalisation which we call sour grapes so his behaviour is not very good, it is escapist.

Linda: It sounds so easy.

Ellis: It is simple, but it is not easy to combat the human condition, which is to be childish more or less all your life: most people are. Just think of the people that you know intimately.

Linda: Well people tell me that's childish or I'm childish. I tell myself that but it is like just a word but I don't think I ever realised what I was doing that was childish.

Ellis: It's a philosophy. I need what I want. I must have my taffy right now.

Linda: So now I'm going to talk to myself and say I don't really need everything I think I need immediately and it might be OK.

Ellis: But you may still want it. We don't want you give up your desire, your value.

Linda: Yeah I may still want it but because I cannot have it then that is the way life really is and maybe I'll even get it later along the way.

Ellis: If I look for it and work for it. You see, the fox gave up.

Linda: I always gave up. I always walked out of every relationship, I said I don't want it.

Ellis: But take this guy you're going with. He is doing this thing that you don't like and let us assume he is wrong and you might even tell him and we'll get back to that, now that is a bad trait but that does not mean that you don't want him at all.

Linda: But you see I looked at that as that's him.

Ellis: But that's *part* of him.

Linda: Yes but I see now what you're saying…

Ellis: But have you asserted yourself, have you calmly un-angrily told him, 'You know dear I wish you wouldn't talk about other women'?

Linda: I have, and he's even said he's sorry, but not only that, you know intellectually I know it is baloney, I know that he is either nervous and just talking or he's reassuring himself or he is testing me. I know he doesn't really care. I also don't know him long enough to really make these demands.

Ellis: Right, so intellectually which means lightly and occasionally you say, 'Well that is the way he is and he isn't even really that way' but emotionally and strongly you say 'He *shouldn't…*'

Linda: I react every time.

Ellis: Because he *shouldn't* do that to a doll like me?

Linda: [*laughs*] I'm either a doll or I'm a shit. That's amazing!

Ellis: But that's interesting. You raise the point that people have two childish philosophies. One is 'I must have everything I want because I want it or the world is a horrible place', which we call low frustration tolerance, demandingness. But the other is 'Unless I do well and win everybody's love as I *must*, I *have to*, then I'm a rotten person, I'm no good'. But these are contradictory philosophies. One says I'm a goddess and the other says I'm a shit.

Linda: Yeah.

Ellis: But they have them, and you could have both and we're trying to get you to see both so that when you're angry at others, you're demanding and commanding that they do what you want that you have to have done and then when you're angry at yourself, you're self-downing, feeling inadequate, you're demanding that you must be perfect and you must always win their love. And isn't that exactly what little children do?

Linda: And then this controlling need goes right along with that.

Ellis: I must control (1) the universe and then (2) myself all my feelings, all my emotions, even when they're doing me in – I *have to*. Not I like to or I want to, that's OK – to want to control the universe, to work to control it, but not completely. You can work to control your feelings, your anger but you don't *have to*, it is the *have to* which does you in.

Linda: Gosh that's really helpful…I…a sort of light went off, I like that idea.

Ellis: You see you have two childish philosophies as most people do, so don't think you're unique in that. Now let me give you another way of doing this because the homework assignment I would give you would be first of all: stay in the situation with him, don't run away, don't cop out like the fox with the grapes. Teach yourself that he has bad traits because he's nervous and other things and I'll stick with it and work on myself and then try to help him have better traits. Don't cop out, stay with it, no matter how uncomfortable it is, stay with it until you get comfortable and then you may decide he's not worth it if he has too many traits you don't like. But temporarily stay with it, bite the bullet. Stay there.

Linda: I like that.

Ellis: Now the second homework is Rational-Emotive Imagery. Let me just show you how to do that. Close your eyes and now imagine the worst, that you told him that you really don't like that kind of stuff and you know he's nervous but you wish he wouldn't tell you about those other women, especially to tell you how good they were and things like that and he keeps doing it, he just ignores you. Now can you vividly imagine that you're assertively saying, 'Now please don't talk about other women' and then he does and sometimes you think that he is almost deliberately doing it. Can you imagine that occurring?

Linda: Oh yeah.

Ellis: How do you honestly feel in your gut as you imagine that?

Linda: I'm mad, I just hate it. I told you not to do it and now…well I really would say 'How dare you?'

Ellis: OK now keep your eyes closed and make yourself really angry and tell me when you've made yourself really angry at him.

Linda: You mean I…

Ellis: Yeah try and be really angry as you are imagining him vividly.

Linda: I mean we've just been over the whole thing and it makes me feel bad and now we're driving down the street and he's saying oh... or he's making a conversation at a dance with a woman across the table or something, a woman who is not with us. And I just cannot believe it I just walk right out of the dance.

Ellis: Make yourself feel very angry and about to withdraw.

Linda: OK. I don't know if I can but I know I would really hate him.

Ellis: Right, make yourself hate him at that moment and envision him and tell me when you are really hating him.

Linda: You see I don't think right there with him I would feel that hatred there so much. I would feel more sick, nauseous.

Ellis: All right but then make yourself feel sick, nauseous. Now you're really feeling sick, nauseous. Yeah. Now keep the same image, he's still doing that, he has not stopped and now you feel only disappointed, only sorry but not sick and not nauseous.

Linda: You're not saying to ignore it.

Ellis: No, no, stay with it, you're still seeing it but make yourself feel sorry, disappointed but not nauseous.

Linda: All right, OK.

Ellis: Now open your eyes. How did you change your feelings?

Linda: I talked to myself.

Ellis: And what did you say?

Linda: I said, it's meaningless, which intellectually I think it is.

Ellis: Right, it is meaningless.

Linda: I don't like it but, but, well you told me before to stick with it and so I've told myself I'm gonna stick with it and maybe it is going to end tomorrow.

Ellis: Oh, OK even though I don't like it I'm gonna stick with it.

Linda: I'll try it another time.

Ellis: OK now what I want you to do for the next 30 days, and you see it only took a few minutes, is imagine the worst, make yourself feel very sick, nauseous or angry whatever you feel and change it to disappointment, sorriness the way you did and other ways which will occur to you. Yours was very good but there are other ways you could tell yourself. Now will you practise that until you feel only sorry, not nauseous, disappointed or angry? If you do that at least once a day at least five minutes a day. In case you don't we'll give you reinforcement. What do you like to do that you do almost every day of the week? Some activity that you enjoy.

Linda: Tennis.

Ellis: Right, no tennis every day until *after* you have done this Rational-Emotive Imagery.

Linda: OK. I see.

Ellis: Then you can play all the tennis you want. And secondly what do you dislike doing, something that you normally avoid doing?

Linda: Too many things I hate, going to the supermarket maybe.

Ellis: OK if by 12 o'clock midnight arrives and you still haven't done your Rational-Emotive Imagery, then you force yourself to the supermarket the next day. But you don't have to go at all if you do the homework.

Linda: OK terrific.

Ellis: Is there any aspect of this anger and self-downing that we haven't brought up right now, any aspect?

Linda: Well, one thing I was thinking was if I carried on and I continued and I didn't feel just disappointed then I would take the choice and I would say to myself well...maybe I cannot live with it and leave?

Ellis: Oh, if you felt very disappointed but not angry, don't leave while you're angry, don't leave while you're nauseous but suppose you're very disappointed, after all you could do better you're a woman who could get other men who aren't this way and suppose you say it is not worth it who needs it? Then you could leave. You're very disappointed, very sorry about him acting this way.

Linda: OK that makes sense, now how about if I could live with this?

Ellis: Oh yes, now let us suppose he really is a doll in many other ways and you are just disappointed about this and he'll always once in a while tell you how great so-and-so was.

Linda: Which is what well...he doesn't dare go that far 'cos I'd throttle him...

Ellis: But he keeps mentioning other women or he'll go over at a dance or something and...

Linda: Yeah or maybe he'll make conversation or think gee they're alone or something.

Ellis: Right now maybe he continues this but has many other good traits then you would convince yourself – that is bad and I wish he wouldn't do it but he will, *too damn bad*. I can get the advantage of being with him and just gracefully lump those things about him which I just don't like.

Linda: Wow, I could do that, eh?

Ellis: Yes you see, and then you widen greatly the number of people you can relate to.

Linda: Oh great that's fabulous.

Ellis: So you work on that then?

Linda: Yeah.

Ellis: Well it was very nice talking to you.

Linda: Thank you.

5

Commentary on Ellis's Interview with Linda

Ellis: What problem would you like to start with?

Again Ellis is problem-focused from the outset.

Linda: Well, I have a problem when my partner talks about previous girl-friends. I feel that I should just ignore it because he is seeing me, but it, it bothers me…it makes me…it bothers me a lot…

Linda does not clearly indicate what her major disturbed feeling is about her partner's behaviour. She refers to being 'bothered', but this is too vague for REBT therapists to work with (see Chapter 1). However, it is common for clients to be vague about their feelings so REBT therapists do need to be skilled at helping their clients to identify their disturbed feelings.

Ellis: Well, how do you feel when he mentions these other women, which of course he doesn't have to, how do you feel?

Ellis quickly picks up on Linda's vague response and asks her to clarify her feelings.

Linda: Mad…[*Ellis*: Yeah so you're angry]…real mad!

Anger can be healthy or unhealthy and often needs to be clarified. However, 'mad' usually refers to unhealthy anger.

Ellis: Because you're telling yourself what, to make yourself angry at him?

It is not clear what, if anything, Linda knows about REBT. Ellis does not endeavour to find out what she knows, nor does he introduce formally REBT's ABC model at this point. He has Linda's A (my partner talks about his previous girlfriends) and her C (anger) so he goes straight to B. Other REBT therapists would take more time to help Linda understand the ABC model and the connections within it (see Dryden, 2002).

Linda: Am I telling myself I do not like myself?

Linda, understandably perhaps, gets her belief wrong.

Ellis: No, no that would make you angry at you, but what are you say-ing about him to make you angry at him?

Ellis shows Linda why that belief would lead to self-anger, but encourages her to try again to identify other anger. Another instance of Ellis giving his client part of the answer, but encouraging her to come up with the other part herself.

Linda: I feel that he should be concentrating on me. Why isn't he think-ing...why aren't you liking *me* why are you even thinking about anyone else?

Linda provides her irrational belief in the form of an unqualified should (see Chapter 1). She then provides a number of rhetorical ques-tions which in this context are often indirect expressions of irrational beliefs.

Ellis: So you're observing that he is not concentrating on you, as far as you can see and then you are feeling very angry at him because he should be concentrating on you – isn't that right?

Notice how careful Ellis is here in presenting the three components of Linda's ABC without mentioning this model. I will do so here:

A = Partner not concentrating on me
B = He should be concentrating on me
C = Anger

Ellis also works with Linda's unqualified should. As I discussed in Chapter 1, I think that it is important to use the qualifier 'absolute' when referring to irrational should since the word 'should' has several different meanings.

Linda: Yeah.
Ellis: And then when you are angry and you know you're angry, how do you feel about you being angry at him?

Ellis is assessing for the presence of a meta-emotional problem.

Linda: I don't know if I think about that, I kind of want to sulk, I'd like to withdraw and not talk to him or run away. If I thought about it I'd probably feel guilty, like I'm acting like a pain in the neck.

Linda's response reveals that there is a hurt component to her anger (sulking is linked most often to hurt). She then mentions guilt, but the fact that she has to think about it indicates that it may not be a problem for her.

Ellis: Right but you don't think about that too much – when you're angry at him, you don't feel guilty?

Linda: Not while I'm with him.

Ellis: No OK but then let us suppose you go away and then you remember you were angry.

Ellis distinguishes between Linda's response to her anger at the time and her response to it later.

Linda: I wouldn't like myself for it.

Linda indicates that while her initial response to her anger is not problematic, her later, more reflective reaction is.

Ellis: Because, and let's start with that, you have two symptoms that most people have. First we'll call it anger, and we will get back to that in a few minutes. And then you feel guilty later when you remember that you were that angry about him and that out of control. Now let's just start with the secondary one the guilt first and let's suppose that you remember and feel guilty now that you felt angry. What are you saying to yourself about being angry that makes you feel guilty? So what do you think that is? What are you telling yourself to make you feel guilty about your anger?

Ellis clearly helps Linda to see the difference between her original problem (anger) and her meta-emotional problem (guilt about her anger). He then unilaterally decides to begin with her meta-emotional problem without explaining why he is doing so or without eliciting her agreement. Ellis rarely pays specific attention to these aspects of the working alliance in his demonstration sessions, preferring to rely on his authority as an expert. Experts know what they are doing and don't need to elicit cooperation from their clients. This is fine with clients who accept the person's authority but may engender resistance in those who don't.

Linda: Well, I should be nice, I should be pleasant when I'm with him and the wonderful person that I am, and instead I feel more like a bitch.

Linda quickly identifies her irrational beliefs.

Ellis: 'I should be nice like all other women would be in this position.' Right but why *must* you be nice?

Ellis reiterates Linda's irrational belief and goes on to challenge it again without explaining to Linda what he is doing and why he is doing it. His challenge is probably an empirical dispute (see Chapter 1).

Linda: That he will not like me maybe if I am not?

Linda's response is incorrect. We know on theoretical grounds that the only correct response is: 'There is no reason why I must be nice.' Ellis knows that Linda's response is wrong and will address it straight away.

Ellis: That's what would be desirable, and most people think in that way. Just because it's desirable to be nice, which let us assume that it is desirable, therefore I must…act desirably. Now does it follow that, even if it is very desirable for you not to be angry with him just to be nice, that you *have* to do what's desirable?

Ellis shows Linda that her response to his dispute of her irrational belief 'I must be nice', namely that he will not like me if I am not nice, is evidence in favour of his rational belief: that it is preferable that I am nice, but I don't always have to be so. Ellis changes tack and focuses on the irrational conclusion 'that you have to do what's desirable' from the rational premise 'it is very desirable for you not to be angry with him, just to be nice' and asks Linda if the former follows from the latter. This is known as a logical dispute of an irrational belief.

Linda: Well no, I guess I don't think about it I just go ahead and get mad.

Linda bypasses the question and argues that she just gets mad rather than thinks.

Ellis: Well you jump, I say you do think about it, you jump from because it is desirable – I shouldn't have done that. At the moment you're focusing on your madness and we'll get back to that. But do you see that even if you went on for the rest of your life foolishly making yourself angry at people like him that that would be allowable? That you could still accept yourself without guilt, do you see that that is so?

Ellis refocuses Linda on her guilt about her anger (her meta-emotional problem) and shows her that she does 'jump' in her thinking from 'because it is desirable I shouldn't have done it'. He then makes the general point that she is 'allowed to' make herself angry for the rest of her life and if she did so, she could accept herself without guilt. Ellis is ambitiously trying to adopt a general rational philosophy before she has adopted a specific rational belief about her anger towards her partner. Ellis's view on this matter can be summed up as: you won't succeed if you don't try.

Linda: By talking to myself a different way and saying that that is OK.

Linda's response is vague and incorrect. She thinks that it is OK to be angry.

Ellis: Not it's OK, because anger isn't OK, you see that would probably ruin your relationships or interrupt your relationship with him, but I'm OK. I can accept me myself even when I act in a non-OK manner such as anger, you see?

As ever, Ellis quickly shows Linda the difference between 'It's OK to be angry', which he is not advocating, and 'I'm OK even if I act in a non-OK manner', which he is advocating.

Linda: All right, I would have to brainwash myself to think that. Let's see…I'm OK even when I get angry and don't like certain things. I don't see it that way, I feel I still see myself as, you know, kind of bitchy and not easygoing.

Linda tries out the rational belief and says that she doesn't feel that way. She is alluding to the insight problem (see Chapter 1) where a client can understand a rational belief but still not believe it.

Ellis: That's OK if you want to see a characteristic or trait of yours as bitchy, but you are not a bitch even when you're bitchy. Do you see why you're still not a bitch even when you are bitchy? Do you see why that is?

Ellis doesn't address the insight problem. Instead he continues with his dispute of Linda's belief, 'I am a bitch for being angry'. He uses his typical tactic of giving the client the answer: 'You are not a bitch even when you are bitchy', and then asking her to explain why this is so.

Linda: I'm OK even though I'm bitchy?
Ellis: And you're not a bitch because a bitch would be completely, thoroughly bitchy all the time.
Linda: Oh, I see, I'm saying one little incident makes me…

Ellis's tactic seems to have paid off as Linda shows that she understands the part–whole error (that a part of a person – bitchiness – cannot define the entire person – a bitch).

Ellis: That's right and also a bitch would be damnable and not OK and so it has two meanings: (1) that I'm thoroughly this way – which is false, and (2) that I am thoroughly damnable because I am sometimes this way. You see your basic demand on yourself is that I *must not* be bitchy *at all* under any conditions. Now is that likely – that you are never going to be bitchy under any conditions?

Here Ellis tries to extend Linda's understanding by showing her that 'I am a bitch for being bitchy' is an over-generalisation and that implicitly she is depreciating or damning herself for her behaviour. He then shows Linda her basic demand, which according to Ellis underpins her self-depreciation belief (see Chapter 1) and empirically challenges this demand. Some REBT therapists would not switch to challenging Linda's demand until they have finished challenging her self-depreciation belief. Ellis tends not to work this way. He will change tack from belief to belief and come back to previously challenged beliefs, trusting that the accumulation of disputes will have its effect. He would regard the more structured approach as needlessly obsessive-compulsive, as I have learned from his feedback to me about my work!

Linda: No, but then maybe I am going to say to myself then 'OK I can go ahead and be a bitch because you know I'm not a total bitch, I'm still a nice person.'

Linda presents a common misconception about self-acceptance: that it does not discourage bad behaviour.

Ellis: Right, but why wouldn't you say that? Let's suppose we get you to accept you with your bitchiness. Now why wouldn't you say 'What difference would it make I'll just go ahead and be bitchy and knock them all off with my bitchiness,' why wouldn't you say that?

Ellis does not correct Linda's misconception, preferring to engage her in correcting it herself.

Linda: Well, because…I'd like to be a little bit easier going, it would make my life easier.

Linda gets the point that self-acceptance would not discourage her from being unbitchy. This is because her preference to be easygoing would constitute her motivation. This shows that if REBT therapists encourage their clients to think in session, sometimes they come to the correct conclusions themselves.

Ellis: That's right because it is *preferable* to be unbitchy not *necessary*, which you are saying it is, and I'm no good if I don't do what is necessary. But it's *preferable* to be unbitchy and even if you accepted you with your bitchiness you'd work against the bitchiness and try to be less bitchy and try to be less angry, which brings us back to the original problem. Now let us go back to the anger, once you accept yourself with your bitchiness, with your anger: it is still unpreferable, still undesirable and so you want to give it up – the anger. Now the anger, he, we'll assume is doing what you said. You could of course be making all this up but I'll assume you are describing correctly and he is gratuitously, needlessly talking about these other women when he could shut his big mouth. Right?

Ellis reinforces Linda's point and then decides to switch back to her original problem. It is clear that Linda still has work to do on her meta-emotional problem, but as this is a demonstration session, Ellis wants to give her *some* help on both her original problem and her meta-emotional problem. When he returns to her anger, he begins by encouraging her to assume that she is correct, that her partner is gratuitously talking about his previous girlfriends. Remember that REBT therapists do this because challenging clients' inferences at A would mean that they would not have access to their irrational beliefs at B.

Linda: Right.
Ellis: He doesn't have to talk about them. OK so what are you saying to you about him when you are angry about him opening his big mouth talking about these other women?

Readers will note that we are back to where we were before Ellis changed tack to work on Linda's meta-emotional problem (see pp. 58–9).

Linda: I don't like him when he is doing that.

Linda provides an other-depreciation belief, albeit in a conversational form.

Ellis: He's doing the wrong thing and I don't like him as a human. He *must not* do that wrong thing. Right? Well why must he not do the wrong thing even if it is wrong?

Ellis takes her other-depreciation belief, links it to her demand about her boyfriend and then challenges this demand.

Linda: Well I thought about that, maybe I need to control the situation, I'm going to set the rules and that's not acceptable.

Rather than answering the question Linda comes up with another demand. Ellis has a choice now. He can keep disputing the first demand about her partner or he can switch to this demand about control.

Ellis: OK so why must you control, it's good to control (probably), but why *must* you, why *need* you control him and the situation?

Ellis decides to switch. Note that he first states Linda's preference and then disputes the demand about the preference.

Linda: I bet we're getting back to I don't like myself if I cannot control the situation.

Linda doesn't answer the question but speculates that this demand leads to self-depreciation.

Ellis: Well partly that is it, if I didn't totally control the situation I would be a pretty rotten person so I think you do have that in there. But there is another reason why people have to control the world aside from self-downing, putting themselves down because of loss of control. Do you know why they demand perfect control?

Ellis acknowledges that demands for control may lead to self-depreciation but he knows they may lead to low frustration tolerance (LFT) – see Chapter 1. Rather than didactically telling Linda about this, he gives her an opportunity to think about this for herself.

Linda: No.
Ellis: Because they *have* to get exactly what they want when they want it.

Since it is clear that Linda does not know the answer to Ellis's question, he answers it for her.

Linda: They have to have get...oh.
Ellis: Therefore I *must* control him and make him say what I want him to say and only what I want him to say.
Linda: So this would go along with something else. If he does not demonstrate and tell me I like you, I really like you and I'm going to change my life tomorrow since I met you. This is the same thing as controlling, as I have to have my way.
Ellis: I have to have my way and also if I don't I'm uncontrolling and a rotten person. You see there are two ideas there: (1) I need what I want, and if I want it I must have it. And then (2), if I am unable to arrange what I want there is something poor and weak about me and I cannot stand me.

Ellis continues to expand on Linda's two irrational beliefs about control – self-depreciation and LFT.

Linda: All right now that first thing you said: if I cannot have what I want because I want it, is that like being a spoilt brat?
Ellis: Well it's like being a brat, I'm not sure you had to be spoilt. You see most children, young children are that way even if they are not spoilt.
Linda: So why aren't most adults like that or is it normal/ordinary?

Ellis: No, it is very common that adults refuse to give up the original childish philosophy and most children, practically all of them have this philosophy: 'Because I want it I should have it. You must give it to me, I should run the universe.' Now some of us decide that we don't run the universe and we don't have to even though it would be nice if we did – and we become mature. But most humans remain immature all their lives and have low frustration tolerance or what I call discomfort anxiety or anxiety about the discomfort of not getting what they want and they don't change their philosophy.

Linda: Oh, I like that.

Ellis: Now you're able to…

Linda: I never thought that was part of growing up that you realise you don't get what you want just because you want it.

Ellis: But isn't it part of growing up, just think of a couple of mature people that you might know – that's if you know any because most people are immature – now don't they, when they get disappointed, when they don't get what they want, don't they conclude something like 'Too bad. I don't need what I want'.

The foregoing exchanges illustrate two things: (a) Ellis's willingness to enter into general discussions of relevant aspects of the human condition even when time is at a premium in a demonstration session; and (b) his adherence to a biological rather than a social learning position of disturbance and his keenness to disabuse clients who espouse a social learning view.

Linda: I don't care really.

Linda confuses a rational conclusion with indifference.

Ellis: Well not I don't care at all, because they still would care but they would be very sorry that…

Ellis corrects her misconception.

Linda: But that is what I have always said.

Ellis: Yeah but that is like the fox and the grapes. The fox cannot get the grapes so he says, 'Who needs the grapes?' But that is wrong. He had better say 'I, the fox, want the grapes and therefore I'll keep jumping or look for other grapes or eat a banana but I don't *need* what I want.' So he ends up with a rationalisation which we call sour grapes so his behaviour is not very good, it is escapist.

Ellis very nicely shows Linda the defensive aspects of indifference when it covers up a demand, by referring to the fox and the grapes fable. Such interventions can be particularly memorable for clients.

Linda: It sounds so easy.

Ellis: It is simple, but it is not easy to combat the human condition, which is to be childish more or less all your life: most people are. Just think of the people that you know intimately.

Ellis shows Linda that there is a world of difference between the ease of understanding the philosophy behind so-called childishness and the difficulty of going against the strong human tendency to cling to such 'childish' beliefs.

Linda: Well people tell me that's childish or I'm childish. I tell myself that but it is like just a word but I don't think I ever realised what I was doing that was childish.

Ellis: It's a philosophy. I need what I want. I must have my taffy right now.

Linda: So now I'm going to talk to myself and say I don't really need everything I think I need immediately and it might be OK.

Ellis: But you may still want it. We don't want you give up your desire, your value.

Ellis reminds Linda that it is perfectly OK to want what she wants, but not, as she now acknowledges, to demand that she has to have it.

Linda: Yeah I may still want it but because I cannot have it then that is the way life really is and maybe I'll even get it later along the way.

Ellis: If I look for it and work for it. You see, the fox gave up.

Ellis shows Linda that her desires will encourage her to look for what she wants and to work for it, and that demands lead people to give up like the fox in the fox and grapes fable.

Linda: I always gave up. I always walked out of every relationship, I said I don't want it.

Linda sees clearly that in the past she gave up on relationships, presumably when her demands were not met.

Ellis: But take this guy you're going with. He is doing this thing that you don't like and let us assume he is wrong and you might even tell him and we'll get back to that, now that is a bad trait but that does not mean that you don't want him at all.

Ellis now applies the general point that they have been discussing to Linda's specific situation with her partner.

Linda: But you see I looked at that as that's him.

Ellis: But that's *part* of him.
Linda: Yes but I see now what you're saying…
Ellis: But have you asserted yourself, have you calmly un-angrily told him, 'You know dear I wish you wouldn't talk about other women'?
Linda: I have, and he's even said he's sorry, but not only that, you know intellectually I know it is baloney, I know that he is either nervous and just talking or he's reassuring himself or he is testing me. I know he doesn't really care. I also don't know him long enough to really make these demands.
Ellis: Right, so intellectually which means lightly and occasionally you say, 'Well that is the way he is and he isn't even really that way' but emotionally and strongly you say 'He *shouldn't*…'
Linda: I react every time.

These exchanges show that assertion and intellectual understanding have not solved Linda's problem.

Ellis: Because he *shouldn't* do that to a doll like me?
Linda: [*laughs*] I'm either a doll or I'm a shit. That's amazing!
Ellis: But that's interesting. You raise the point that people have two childish philosophies. One is 'I must have everything I want because I want it or the world is a horrible place', which we call low frustration tolerance, demandingness. But the other is 'Unless I do well and win everybody's love as I *must*, I *have to*, then I'm a rotten person, I'm no good'. But these are contradictory philosophies. One says I'm a goddess and the other says I'm a shit.

Ellis shows that it is possible to hold two contradictory irrational demanding philosophies, one based on a god-like LFT the other based on self-depreciation.

Linda: Yeah.
Ellis: But they have them, and you could have both and we're trying to get you to see both so that when you're angry at others, you're demanding and commanding that they do what you want that you have to have done and then when you're angry at yourself, you're self-downing, feeling inadequate, you're demanding that you must be perfect and you must always win their love. And isn't that exactly what little children do?
Linda: And then this controlling need goes right along with that.
Ellis: I must control (1) the universe and then (2) myself, all my feelings, all my emotions, even when they're doing me in – I *have to*. Not I like to or I want to, that's OK – to want to control the universe, to work to control it, but not completely. You can work to control your feelings, your anger but you don't *have to*, it is the *have to* which does you in.

Linda: Gosh that's really helpful…I…a sort of light went off, I like that idea.
Ellis: You see you have two childish philosophies as most people do, so don't think you're unique in that.

Ellis continues with this general conceptualisation of Linda's problems until she really seems to understand his point.

> Now let me give you another way of doing this because the homework assignment I would give you would be first of all: stay in the situation with him, don't run away, don't cop out like the fox with the grapes. Teach yourself that he has bad traits because he's nervous and other things and I'll stick with it and work on myself and then try to help him have better traits. Don't cop out, stay with it, no matter how uncomfortable it is, stay with it until you get comfortable and then you may decide he's not worth it if he has too many traits you don't like. But temporarily stay with it, bite the bullet. Stay there.

Ellis now becomes practical and suggests what is known as a stay-in-there homework assignment where Linda stays in the situation with her partner and learns not to disturb herself about him and when she has done that she is in a better position to judge the viability of the relationship. He suggests this assignment because of her tendency to walk away from relationships. My own inclination would be to encourage Linda to be more specific about the irrational beliefs that she needs to challenge to allow her to remain in the situation, namely her demand that her partner not discuss other women, and to be more concrete in helping her to do this.

Linda: I like that.

Ellis is now going to teach Linda a technique called Rational-Emotive Imagery which I discussed in Chapter 1.

Ellis: Now the second homework is Rational-Emotive Imagery. Let me just show you how to do that. Close your eyes and now imagine the worst, that you told him that you really don't like that kind of stuff and you know he's nervous but you wish he wouldn't tell you about those other women, especially to tell you how good they were and things like that and he keeps doing it, he just ignores you. Now can you vividly imagine that you're assertively saying, 'Now please don't talk about other women' and then he does and sometimes you think that he is almost deliberately doing it. Can you imagine that occurring?
Linda: Oh yeah.

Ellis: How do you honestly feel in your gut as you imagine that?

Linda: I'm mad, I just hate it. I told you not to do it and now...well I really would say 'How dare you?'

Ellis: OK now keep your eyes closed and make yourself really angry and tell me when you've made yourself really angry at him.

Linda: You mean I...

Ellis: Yeah try and be really angry as you are imagining him vividly.

Linda: I mean we've just been over the whole thing and it makes me feel bad and now we're driving down the street and he's saying oh... or he's making a conversation at a dance with a woman across the table or something, a woman who is not with us. And I just cannot believe it. I just walk right out of the dance.

Ellis: Make yourself feel very angry and about to withdraw.

Linda: OK. I don't know if I can but I know I would really hate him.

Ellis: Right, make yourself hate him at that moment and envision him and tell me when you are really hating him.

Linda: You see I don't think right there with him I would feel that hatred there so much. I would feel more sick, nauseous.

Ellis: All right but then make yourself feel sick, nauseous. Now you're really feeling sick, nauseous. Yeah. Now keep the same image, he's still doing that, he has not stopped and now you feel only disappointed, only sorry but not sick and not nauseous.

Linda: You're not saying to ignore it.

Ellis: No, no, stay with it, you're still seeing it but make yourself feel sorry, disappointed but not nauseous.

Linda: All right, OK.

Ellis: Now open your eyes. How did you change your feelings?

Linda: I talked to myself.

Ellis: And what did you say?

Linda: I said, it's meaningless, which intellectually I think it is.

Ellis: Right, it is meaningless.

Linda: I don't like it but, but, well you told me before to stick with it and so I've told myself I'm gonna stick with it and maybe it is going to end tomorrow.

The problem with Ellis's version of REI is that it depends on the client changing her feelings by changing her irrational beliefs to rational beliefs. What Linda has come up with is rational in a vague sort of way, but it is not as specific as it needs to be and not as focused on her partner's tendency to talk about other women as it needs to be.

Ellis: Oh, OK even though I don't like it I'm gonna stick with it.

Linda: I'll try it another time.

Ellis: OK now what I want you to do for the next 30 days, and you see it only took a few minutes, is imagine the worst, make yourself feel very sick, nauseous or angry whatever you feel and change it to disappointment, sorriness the way you did and other ways which will occur to you. Yours was very good but there are other ways you could tell yourself. Now will you practise that until you feel only sorry, not nauseous, disappointed or angry? If you do that at least once a day at least five minutes a day: in case you don't we'll give you reinforcement. What do you like to do that you do almost every day of the week? Some activity that you enjoy.

Linda: Tennis.

Ellis: Right, no tennis every day until *after* you have done this Rational-Emotive Imagery.

Linda: OK. I see.

Ellis: Then you can play all the tennis you want. And secondly what do you dislike doing, something that you normally avoid doing?

Linda: Too many things I hate, going to the supermarket maybe.

Ellis: OK if by 12 o'clock midnight arrives and you still haven't done your Rational-Emotive Imagery, then you force yourself to the supermarket the next day. But you don't have to go at all if you do the homework.

Linda: OK terrific.

Ellis invariably suggests this technique in case the client doesn't do REI for homework. Do the REI and you can have your reward and avoid the penalty. Don't do it and forgo your reward and apply the penalty. Of course, the client can decide not to do the REI, but still have the reward and not apply the penalty. However, at least Ellis is addressing the issue of homework non-compliance.

Ellis: Is there any aspect of this anger and self-downing that we haven't brought up right now, any aspect?

Linda: Well, one thing I was thinking was if I carried on and I continued and I didn't feel just disappointed then I would take the choice and I would say to myself well…maybe I cannot live with it and leave?

Ellis: Oh, if you felt very disappointed but not angry, don't leave while you're angry, don't leave while you're nauseous but suppose you're very disappointed, after all you could do better you're a woman who could get other men who aren't this way and suppose you say it is not worth it who needs it? Then you could leave. You're very disappointed, very sorry about him acting this way.

In response to Linda's question, Ellis reiterates a point that he made earlier: that the best time to decide whether or not to leave a relationship is when you are not disturbed about it, but healthily disappointed about it.

Linda: OK that makes sense, now how about if I could live with this?

Ellis: Oh yes, now let us suppose he really is a doll in many other ways and you are just disappointed about this and he'll always once in a while tell you how great so-and-so was.

Linda: Which is what well...he doesn't dare go that far 'cos I'd throttle him...

Ellis: But he keeps mentioning other women or he'll go over at a dance or something and...

Linda: Yeah or maybe he'll make conversation or think gee they're alone or something.

Ellis: Right now maybe he continues this but has many other good traits then you would convince yourself – that is bad and I wish he wouldn't do it but he will, *too damn bad*. I can get the advantage of being with him and just gracefully lump those things about him which I just don't like.

Ellis shows Linda that if she decides to stay with her partner because the advantages of doing so outweigh the reasons for leaving then if he continues talking about past girlfriends she can tolerate it without resentment because it is worth doing so.

Linda: Wow, I could do that, eh?

Linda resonates with this approach.

Ellis: Yes you see, and then you widen greatly the number of people you can relate to.

Linda: Oh great that's fabulous.

Ellis: So you work on that then?

Linda: Yeah.

Ellis: Well it was very nice talking to you.

Linda: Thank you.

Feedback

What follows is a brief interview carried out with Linda after the session, designed to gauge her reactions to the session. I will again add my comments at various points.

Interviewer: I'd like to get a little feedback on how you experienced the session and how you liked working with Dr Ellis.

Linda: I really loved it. I felt that...I really felt that I could work things out already and I haven't even done my homework, you know that I have a concrete, a concrete direction to go in and I feel very positive about the dilemma because I had seen it before as maybe hopeless at times. Well I feel a lot more positive about it.

Linda indicates that Ellis has given her a 'concrete direction to go in' counteracting her previous feelings of hopelessness about the issue.

Interviewer: So you feel a lot more optimistic about being able to get a handle on it. What in particular, what insights were most important that you plan on trying outside?

Linda: Well I think the thing that hit home a lot was the thing about being childish in the sense that if you don't like something you just run away, which I have always done and kind of known it's not a good thing to do, but I kind of went on doing it. Then I always knew that I act childishly and people have told me and it did not mean anything but now he has said that sticking it out even when we don't like it or are angry about something is being mature. And so now I'm going to say to myself that I'm going to stick there and stay there until I can get to the point where I am not frustrated – I am just disappointed. It's like the lights went on and now I could work out – I might have been getting rid of a lot of nice things. Because I cannot have exactly what I want when I want it then I get rid of it. Now I can say, 'Gee I don't have to get rid of it maybe I'll give it another try and maybe there'll be something there.'

Linda indicates that it was the discussion about childishness and walking away from situations that had the biggest impact on her. She sees the value of staying in situations until she is disappointed. She is still not very clear that she can best do this by disputing her demand that she must get what she wants; nor is her rational belief, which should be: 'I very much want to get what I want, but I really don't have to get it', expressed as clearly as I would want Linda to express it.

Interviewer: Build up your emotional muscle?

Linda: Yeah.

Interviewer: What was your reaction to Dr Ellis as a therapist, were you comfortable with him?

Linda: I was, it seemed a little, you know formal like I didn't...I don't know...let me see, what do I mean there? I guess I felt a little nervous, it was kind of 'businesslike'. It was very direct and to the point and very helpful so how could I not like it?

This is interesting. Ellis does not set out to have a warm relationship with his clients. Linda shows that a 'businesslike' relationship is not an obstacle to being helped.

Interviewer: You felt understood...? He was tuned in to your emotions and your feelings?

Linda: Yeah definitely, I felt he stayed right on my problem and I felt I kept on taking one more step and I really feel wonderful about it.

As Linda shows, Ellis is both businesslike *and* empathic. The former does not exclude the latter.

Interviewer: OK. Thank you very much. Is there anything you can think of that you would like to add in terms of your reaction to the session?

Linda: Well I do like this type of, his way of therapy, you know I've read something about it and it makes a lot of sense and I am real enthusiastic when I see it applied to my own life and I feel I've got it right in my hands something I can do.

Interviewer: Well it is easier said than done, it takes practice.

Linda: I know, well I'm going to do those homework things and I'll let you know in 30 days.

Interviewer: OK. Well we may get in touch with you, thank you.

Linda: Thank you.

6

Ellis's Interview with Lucy

Ellis: Hello, Lucy. What problem would you like to begin with?

Lucy: Well, I'm concerned with the way I've been dealing with my feelings in relation to the death of my daughter.

Ellis: Yeah. When did your daughter die?

Lucy: Two years ago.

Ellis: And how old was she?

Lucy: She had just turned 19.

Ellis: Oh. And it suddenly happened?

Lucy: Yes. She had gone to Toronto and she was in a car crash. She died instantly.

Ellis: And you were quite shocked when this happened?

Lucy: I was totally, totally numb. It was just inconceivable, that was my reaction. I just could not believe this had happened.

Ellis: Because she was in such good health, and so alive?

Lucy: Yeah, yeah.

Ellis: Was she your only child?

Lucy: No, we have another girl who is 18 now.

Ellis: Yeah.

Lucy: And she was quite close to her sister.

Ellis: So she was shocked, too?

Lucy: She was.

Ellis: And how did your husband take it?

Lucy: Well, my husband was absolutely beside himself. Up to that time he had always been a very strong, very sensible, very organised person, not terribly emotional. I thought I was the emotional one, and he was absolutely distraught. Umm, he was able to continue working but he just cried all the time, umm, blamed himself.

Ellis: He blamed himself? For letting her go?

Lucy: Because he had given final permission and the plane fare.

Ellis: Yeah.

Lucy: Uh-huh. I told him, 'Look, I was the one who had also tried to convince her' because our daughter had won me over, you know, 'It would be a wonderful vacation and I've worked hard, I deserve it.' She pleaded a convincing case. So I told my husband, 'Well, you know, if you are blaming yourself then you should also be blaming me and I should be blaming me.' Which I did, for a long time.

Ellis: For letting her go?

Lucy: For letting her go, right. Because we knew that if we had said 'No you may not go', that she would have been forced to abide by our wishes because she had no money and, er, when my husband reacted in this way I just felt, and this is part of my problem, that I had to be the strong one. I had to just keep things running as normally as possible, I was terribly concerned about my daughter, I tried not to cry in front of her because I didn't want to upset her. It had been such a horrible thing for her too. Because she had always been a very fearful child too. And here her sister, her only sibling, died like that. So I just felt that I was caught up in this situation where I was trying not to upset anybody, you know and I was walking around like a mummy half the time...

Ellis: So you were holding back from your feelings because you were afraid if you let them go your husband and your daughter would be even more upset?

Lucy: Yeah. And my parents. We had elderly grandparents to consider. Umm, and I'm not saying that I never felt this acutely, I did, but not terribly frequently because I think I just didn't let myself.

Ellis: Yup.

Lucy: I used to dream about her all the time, I still do, umm...

Ellis: Well, many people don't feel temporarily because as you say they don't let themselves feel but then later it comes out, and how do you think you feel now when it comes to mind?

Lucy: This is my problem, you know. I feel that, umm, I am not reacting the way a normal mother who idolised...I feel that way about both of the girls, I idolised them. I thought how is it possible for me to be functioning, to be doing normal things, er, to even be able to go to the cemetery and not be totally shattered.

Ellis: So you're guilty because you're not reacting the way you think a normal mother should?

Lucy: I think so, I really do.

Ellis: Well, let's suppose, for the sake of discussion, that you really are, and actually there are many mothers who would react this way, especially after two years, they go back. First they hold themselves in and then they go back to their preoccupations and lives. You're going to school now, is that right?

Lucy: Well, I'm working and writing.

Ellis: Yup. So you're working and writing, and you have the regular duties of a mother, you have your other child who is still at home...[*Lucy*: Yes] and you're a wife. So many would do that but let's suppose that many would not [*Lucy*: Uh-hmm] that many would be still distraught and wouldn't be able to work. Now why do you have to be exactly like the so-called normal mother who would be despairing and disorganised by her daughter's death two years ago?

Lucy: I don't know, you know. Part of it has to do with the fact that for a while I was attending a bereaved parents' group.

Ellis: Yeah.

Lucy: And, er, I would sit there, and these people would be rending their hair, rending their clothing, you know. And their attitude seemed to be that the whole world out there had to make some accommodation to the fact that their child had died.

Ellis: Right.

Lucy: And I never expected that. You know, I just felt that I, you know.

Ellis: But weren't they a bit grandiose in their expectations that if they [Lucy: Oh yeah] rended their hair and tore their shirts and dresses, that the whole world should make an adjustment. Wasn't that a bit grandiose?

Lucy: I thought so.

Ellis: And wasn't the group encouraging them to do that, to let it all out, to let their feelings out?

Lucy: Yeah. That was why I stopped going to the group after a number of months.

Ellis: Well, I was just gonna say, don't forget that those groups, because they're a certain way, and I'm not sure about your group, but it sounds like one of these really expressive groups, they have a selective group that keeps going to them. But people like you, you dropped out and you were comparing yourself to those who stayed and you were saying 'I'm abnormal compared to them'.

Lucy: M'mm.

Ellis: Meaning unusual.

Lucy: Yeah. That's exactly it.

Ellis: But let's suppose you are. Why is that bad? That you're not as disorganised and rending your shirt and tearing your hair as much as they? Why is that a bad kind of reaction?

Lucy: Well I don't know. But the thing is that I remember that when she was little I used to sometimes have these nightmares that something awful happened to her and it would be so hideous and I would wake up and realise that it had been a dream and it was such an incredible relief. And here the nightmare became a reality [Ellis: Yeah] and I thought how can I deal with this? How is it possible?

Ellis: But you did deal with this.

Lucy: In my own way, I guess.

Ellis: And isn't that very common among us humans? That we think the worst thing that would happen and we think of ourselves as unable to deal with it?

Lucy: Yes.

Ellis: But when an accident happens and we almost get into one or there is a crisis, we almost do deal with it much better than we imagined at the worst. Isn't that a very common trait?

Lucy: Well, I suppose it is.

Ellis: And I don't think you're accepting this fact, that most people, after two years, do adjust to the death of their daughter, no matter how shocked they are and they go on with their lives.

Lucy: Well you know, the thing is that this pattern began way before the two years...[*Ellis:* Right] I was going about my business almost two weeks later. Umm, I couldn't deal with certain things, I just could not bring myself to do for a few weeks, I could not go to the supermarket. I just didn't wanna see anybody and deal with that. But shortly after that, I did. I forced myself.

Ellis: And you know why that was good, that you forced yourself to do that?

Lucy: Umm, it was a matter of emotional survival, I think.

Ellis: That's right, emotional survival not only practical survival because you had better do some of those things. You still were a mother, you still were a wife, and therefore you'd better do them. But also when we distract ourselves into any concerted activity, anything that really preoccupies us, then temporarily, not permanently, we forget about the horrors of life and the things that have happened to us and we're able to control our own feelings and be much more accepting of reality. Now if you had the time and you didn't do anything with it and you mainly kept thinking and thinking about the death of your daughter, the death of your daughter, and how awful that was, you would have been much more shattered and much less effective. So that wasn't a bad thing to do, to become preoccupied and force yourself even uncomfortably to do things. We often give that homework assignment in therapy to people, to force themselves to do something that's uncomfortable and then it becomes easier to do it. And you did that kind of thing for a while and I think it was a very good thing even though your group probably didn't approve of it, did they?

Lucy: Well, they didn't express it as approval, really, they would say things like well, you know, whatever's your way is fine, it's your way and we all have our own way. It's the feeling that I got, though, that my way did not seem to be the predominant way [*laughing a little*] and that way just didn't feel right for me.

Ellis: Well, but that's ironic what you're saying because it was your way. It probably was right for you but not [*Lucy:* But not, yeah] for them. Now you seem to feel uncomfortable that you're in a minority.

Lucy: I was, yeah. I was, yes.

Ellis: And that's good, right? Now why is it so bad, to be in a minority and do things your way, grieve in your way, rather than their way. What's so unusual or abnormal about that?

Lucy: Well you see, that is the basic problem that I have had. I've been in therapy for two years and I think it's on the way out but I've always had this problem whereby others' wishes, others' feelings seem to take predominance over mine.

Ellis: Because, if I do my things my way and put my wishes and feelings first, what are you concluding – that's so bad?

Lucy: Well, the…the deviation must be wrong. Something like that.

Ellis: And that makes me what kind of a person if I deviate and I'm wrong?

Lucy: Oh – a bad person.

Ellis: Now how does that follow? Let's just assume for the sake of discussion that you're not only unusual in some trait such as grieving for your daughter but abnormal, really pathological and deliberately assume the worst that that is so. I don't think that was so. I think you reacted in a quite healthy though unusual manner. But let's suppose you were wrong and pathological. How would that behaviour, that wrongness, make you a bad person?

Lucy: Well, sensibly speaking, it wouldn't [laughing].

Ellis: But in your head?

Lucy: Emotionally, I guess, I, you know, I felt that if I did not jive with the others, that there was something wrong with me.

Ellis: Because I should be and do what? What's your demand on yourself?

Lucy: Like everybody else. Quote, 'normal'. Whatever.

Ellis: Well, let us even suppose it would be desirable – which I don't happen to agree with – you being like everybody else because then you'd just be like them, you wouldn't be you, but let's suppose it were desirable. Why do you have to act desirably?

Lucy: Ah, well, that dates back to the way I was brought up [laughing]. Umm, I now realise that why should I give a shit, you know, it took me a long time, my family…

Ellis: But now wait a minute. It wasn't the way you were brought up, that's a false perception. A lot of people, especially psychoanalysts believe that, that the way you were brought up you adopt, and therefore you make it your own. [Lucy: Mm-hmm] But we know if a hundred or a thousand children were brought up exactly the same way as you, they wouldn't be as great conformists all the same as you. Isn't that true? [Lucy: Uh-huh] Now, therefore, what was there about you to begin with that made you listen so carefully to your mother?

Lucy: I was always very passive. [Ellis: Ahh!] And in my marriage I was. My husband took over and I absorbed his opinions about things.

Ellis: Because if I refuse to go along with people and have their approval, what does that mean about me as a person?

Lucy: Oh, as a person, I'm not sure about that, but I know that it was always caught up in my mind with having to suffer some sort of punishment.

Ellis: I deserve punishment if I do the unusual wrong thing and they don't approve of it, is that right?

Lucy: Right.

Ellis: So, can you see that this was the philosophy which you had as a young child, which was native to you, natural to you, that you brought to the original situation, and that you're bringing now?

Lucy: Yeah.

Ellis: To this situation. The philosophy that I come second [*Lucy*: Yeah] and other people's approval comes first. [*Lucy*: Yeah] Now let's question that. Why do you have to be second to other people's approval and why must you win their love and acceptance?

Lucy: Well, here again, it's difficult because I no longer feel that I do. I feel that I'm coming out of that now but it was a way of creating a peaceful, no-waves type of picture.

Ellis: Which I had to have?

Lucy: Yes.

Ellis: You see you put in the *had to have* there. But I think you are coming out of it. You sound much better than you were, certainly as a child [*Lucy*: Yeah] and as a young wife and even two years ago but how could you really, solidly get on to it because at times you sink back. You say I'm not mourning, I'm not grieving the way others do, there must be something wrong with me, you feel guilty. Now how can you solidly accept you even if you were quite unusual and not doing what the normal or average person does?

Lucy: Well, I could simply tell myself that there's no question that I am grieving for her [*Ellis*: Right), it may not be the way that someone else might.

Ellis: Right.

Lucy: But I, there's no question that I am.

Ellis: And I'm entitled to what? What are you entitled to?

Lucy: Well, to do, to deal with it in my own way. However that way may be.

Ellis: And however people think of me for having my own way. You see? Now if you would really go over that every time you feel guilty or depressed, not grieving and sad about your daughter, because from time to time for the rest of your life you're going to remember this, or read about another accident or something like that, or you'll meet one of her friends, and you'll feel very sad because you believe correctly isn't it most unfortunate that I lost my daughter who was so alive [*Lucy*: Mm-hmm], so good in her way, and now she doesn't exist so you'll feel sad, but we don't want you to feel guilty or depressed because depression usually means: 'The sadness should not, *must* not exist and I can't bear it', and you've shown that you can bear it in fact you've borne it remarkably well and when you don't get guilty about your reactions then you do fine in spite of this real tragedy with your daughter.

Lucy: You know, there was, there's something else that happened as a result of what happened to my daughter. And all these things have happened over the past two years. Umm, my way of dealing with what happened to my daughter affected my marriage. [*Ellis*: Right] Right now I'm separated. What happened was that, er, I just could not seem to reach out to my husband in the way that he seemed to need. I was just caught up in my own, holding myself together. [*Ellis*: Right] And so what eventually happened was that he started to have an affair with his 23-year-old secretary, which I learned about last January, which absolutely blew me apart...

Ellis: Which *you* blew you apart because *you* took it too seriously. What did you tell yourself when he had that affair?

Lucy: Well, what it told me was that he was a shit. Really, that was how I felt. I felt that, and I know this sounds like self-pity but I just felt like a dying horse who he had to supply the last few kicks to, to finish the job.

Ellis: So you were saying, how could he do that to me?

Lucy: Yes.

Ellis: In my hour of need.

Lucy: Right.

Ellis: So that is what you told yourself and you felt self-pity and anger at him as a result.

Lucy: Extreme anger. And in that case I didn't seem to have any trouble expressing my feelings, er, of course his response was look, you know, after Sarah died, I just didn't know where to turn and she was there and she comforted me and one thing led to another, you know that whole thing. And that was his view of the situation, in fact right now he claims to have terminated it and, er, he wants to come home.

Ellis: Right.

Lucy: Umm.

Ellis: And how do you feel about that?

Lucy: I feel that all of my anger and hurt and resentment have not really been acknowledged by him. He hasn't really made me feel that I have a right to those feelings. He's tried even to make me assume partial responsibility for this affair.

Ellis: Well, but isn't that because he is defensive and if he thought you were justifiably angry and hurt then he would put himself down so [*Lucy*: Yeah] he wanted to think that you were 100 per cent responsible but to a degree you are responsible for your hurt and your anger, you know why that is. You're not responsible for what he did. Your anger comes from you and do you know why it comes from you rather than from what he did?

Lucy: Well, maybe because I feel that, umm, this is something he did to me.

Ellis: And should not have done to me, especially under those conditions.

Lucy: Yes.

Ellis: But he should have done that to you. You know why he should have done that to you?

Lucy: Because he did it [*laughing*].

Ellis: That's right. That's his nature.

Lucy: [*laughing*] Yeah.

Ellis: You see, now if you fully accept that, and we're not apologising for him or condoning what he did, especially when he tried to blame you for everything. But if that's his nature, that's his nature and that what he did isn't totally him, yeah? [*Lucy*: Mm-hmm] He has lots of other traits so if you would accept him, but not what he did then you would feel sorry and displeased with his behaviour but you would lose the anger at him. You see if you could fully accept him as a fallible human who did the wrong thing and tried to put everything on you and that's very wrong but he is a person who did a bad thing rather than a bad person, then again you wouldn't feel angry. You see that that's correct?

Lucy: Well, I do, and I would have been able to somehow transcend that business if he had put a clean end to it, when he said he was going to which was about seven months ago, she works for him. [*Ellis*: Yeah] And he had said well listen, I'm going to end it and she'll be leaving the office in a few weeks, just give me some time. Well, weeks went and months went. Now she's leaving, presumably in two weeks. Now during the seven months while we were living apart and I was giving him time and we were continuing to see each other because he wanted to come and visit our daughter and all that, and also I could feel the hurt and rage and resentment just building and building, and I was saying to myself well, it's been seven months, you know, when? And…and he would say things like, I'm dealing with it my own way and when I am ready, she will go, as though I didn't matter, you know?

Ellis: Right, and I hear you saying (1) he took too long and (2) he didn't let me matter and he *should* not, *must* not act that way. Is that right?

Lucy: Yes.

Ellis: And again, shouldn't he act the way he indubitably does?

Lucy: Well, apparently there was no other way that he did act.

Ellis: Right. And if you would accept him with that bad behaviour and I'm again not apologising for his behaviour or saying that it's good but presume he promised you and then didn't go through with his promises. That's bad behaviour. He was not trustworthy.

Lucy: That is the key. Yeah.

Ellis: But he is a human with untrustworthy behaviour, he's not a lousy, totally untrustworthy human. Do you see the difference?

Lucy: Yes, but then, can you have a relationship with someone who you feel is untrustworthy?

Ellis: If you were un-angry you would decide that. [*Lucy*: Mm-hmm] If you got rid of your anger and your hurt, your self-pity, then you would decide whether it's worth it and that's what we'd better finally decide in life, seeing that a human acts a bad way in our eyes, we don't like it, the way he acts, now does he have another, other compensatory trait?

Lucy: Oh yeah. Sure, he has many.

Ellis: All right. Now if you are un-angry but still displeased with that particular behaviour and still not trusting him totally, because you didn't trust him and you couldn't trust him in that respect and you would finally decide whether it was worth it.

Lucy: Hmmm.

Ellis: So the problem from an emotional standpoint, from a Rational Emotive Behaviour Therapy standpoint, is first to get rid of your self-blaming about your husband and especially about your child, that you contributed to her going away, to accept you totally, even though you may have done the unwise thing in letting her go because you could've stopped her but don't forget that could have had hassles and problems too because then she would have been upset about being stopped.

Lucy: Yeah.

Ellis: But let's just suppose the worst and you did the wrong thing. You are a human who made an error but by the same token your husband, under great duress, under great stress because he was very upset about the child, he had this affair, he lied to you. He prolonged it way beyond what he could've, therefore he is a human who did the wrong thing, but he is not a rotten human. No human is rotten, you know why no human is a rotten person?

Lucy: I don't know if I agree [*laughing*].

Ellis: Why?

Lucy: Umm...

Ellis: Because?

Lucy: You're naming the behaviour and attributing it to the person.

Ellis: And we're saying the person is responsible for the behaviour so we're not saying you're not responsible for what you did or that your husband isn't responsible for what he did. But we're saying that a human has so many behaviours, hundreds, thousands in his or her lifetime, that the behaviours change, the human as a whole changes, and too bad, that's the way all humans are, fallible, screwed up, and we don't have to be with them but we'd better first accept ourselves and then, and then later decide whether it's worth it, whether they have so many poor behaviours [*Lucy*: Yeah] that being with them isn't worth it. Now, if you would do that, first totally accept you and then totally accept your husband, but not the way he acts, I'm not saying that, then you can make your own hedonic calculus to see whether it's more pleasurable being with him than not, and then you'll finally decide and if you stay with him fine and if you don't that's OK too, if you see what I mean. [*Lucy*: Yeah] So I want you to give that some thought. Your home-work assignment will be to see that you create your own hurt and your own guilt especially about your daughter, and you can always give that up by totally accepting you. And your husband. He does his bad things but you make yourself angry at him and then you don't know what to do. So that you can de-anger, get rid of your anger at him then decide later what to do. Now if you would work on that then you won't easily make a decision, it'll still be difficult to make a decision, but you will go about your life and be able to make a decision easier. [*Lucy*: Hm-hmm] So if you wanna try what we've been talking about...

Lucy: Yeah.

Ellis: OK. It was certainly good talking with you.

Lucy: It was good talking to you too. Thank you.

7

Commentary on Ellis's Interview with Lucy

Ellis: Hello, Lucy. What problem would you like to begin with?

Ellis's now familiar problem-focused opener.

Lucy: Well, I'm concerned with the way I've been dealing with my feelings in relation to the death of my daughter.

Ellis: Yeah. When did your daughter die?

Lucy: Two years ago.

Ellis: And how old was she?

Lucy: She had just turned 19.

Ellis: Oh. And it suddenly happened?

Lucy: Yes. She had gone to Toronto and she was in a car crash. She died instantly.

Ellis: And you were quite shocked when this happened?

Lucy: I was totally, totally numb. It was just inconceivable, that was my reaction. I just could not believe this had happened.

Ellis: Because she was in such good health, and so alive?

Lucy: Yeah, yeah.

Ellis: Was she your only child?

Lucy: No, we have another girl who is 18 now.

Ellis: Yeah.

Lucy: And she was quite close to her sister.

Ellis: So she was shocked, too?

Lucy: She was.

Ellis: And how did your husband take it?

Lucy: Well, my husband was absolutely beside himself. Up to that time he had always been a very strong, very sensible, very organised person, not terribly emotional. I thought I was the emotional one, and he was absolutely distraught. Umm, he was able to continue working but he just cried all the time, umm, blamed himself.

Ellis: He blamed himself? For letting her go?

Lucy: Because he had given final permission and the plane fare.

Ellis: Yeah.

Lucy: Uh-huh. I told him, 'Look, I was the one who had also tried to convince her,' because our daughter had won me over, you know, 'It would be a wonderful vacation and I've worked hard, I deserve it.'

She pleaded a convincing case. So I told my husband, 'Well, you know, if you are blaming yourself then you should also be blaming me and I should be blaming me.' Which I did, for a long time.

Ellis: For letting her go?

Lucy: For letting her go, right. Because we knew that if we had said 'No you may not go', that she would have been forced to abide by our wishes because she had no money and, er, when my husband reacted in this way I just felt, and this is part of my problem, that I had to be the strong one. I had to just keep things running as normally as possible, I was terribly concerned about my daughter, I tried not to cry in front of her because I didn't want to upset her. It had been such a horrible thing for her too. Because she had always been a very fearful child too. And here her sister, her only sibling, died like that. So I just felt that I was caught up in this situation where I was trying not to upset anybody, you know and I was walking around like a mummy half the time…

Ellis: So you were holding back from your feelings because you were afraid if you let them go your husband and your daughter would be even more upset?

Lucy: Yeah. And my parents. We had elderly grandparents to consider. Umm, and I'm not saying that I never felt this acutely, I did, but not terribly frequently because I think I just didn't let myself.

Ellis: Yup.

Lucy: I used to dream about her all the time, I still do, umm…

Ellis: Well, many people don't feel temporarily because as you say they don't let themselves feel but then later it comes out, and how do you think you feel now when it comes to mind?

Up to now Ellis has been content for Lucy to express herself in her own way, asking pertinent questions to get the context clear in his mind. This is probably because of the delicate nature of the subject matter. Throughout this portion of the interview, Ellis's tone of voice has been gentle and subdued, which may come as a surprise to some. Having understood the context, Ellis brings Lucy back to the present.

Lucy: This is my problem, you know. I feel that, umm, I am not reacting the way a normal mother who idolised…I feel that way about both of the girls, I idolised them. I thought how is it possible for me to be functioning, to be doing normal things, er, to even be able to go to the cemetery and not be totally shattered.

Ellis: So you're guilty because you're not reacting the way you think a normal mother should?

Note how concise Ellis is here. He summarises Lucy's problem in one sentence.

Lucy: I think so, I really do.

Ellis: Well, let's suppose, for the sake of discussion, that you really are, and actually there are many mothers who would react this way, especially after two years, they go back. First they hold themselves in and then they go back to their preoccupations and lives. You're going to school now, is that right?

Lucy: Well, I'm working and writing.

Ellis: Yup. So you're working and writing, and you have the regular duties of a mother, you have your other child who is still at home… [*Lucy*: Yes] and you're a wife. So many would do that but let's suppose that many would not [*Lucy*: Uh-hmm] that many would be still distraught and wouldn't be able to work. Now why do you have to be exactly like the so-called normal mother who would be despairing and disorganised by her daughter's death two years ago?

What Ellis does here is very interesting. He encourages Lucy to assume 'for the sake of discussion' that she isn't reacting like a normal mother. This is, of course, the standard REBT tactic of encouraging the clients to assume that A is true so as to facilitate the assessment of the irrational beliefs at B. However, by saying to Lucy that many mothers would react like her, he is also normalising her experience. Yet, having identified her guilt-creating irrational belief, he once again immediately goes on to dispute it. But note his use of the term 'so-called' in his dispute. Even here he is calling into question how realistic Lucy's standard is.

Lucy: I don't know, you know. Part of it has to do with the fact that for a while I was attending a bereaved parents' group.

This probably explains the source of her standard.

Ellis: Yeah.

Lucy: And, er, I would sit there, and these people would be rending their hair, rending their clothing, you know. And their attitude seemed to be that the whole world out there had to make some accommodation to the fact that their child had died.

Ellis: Right.

Lucy: And I never expected that. You know, I just felt that I, you know.

Ellis: But weren't they a bit grandiose in their expectations that if they [*Lucy*: Oh yeah] rended their hair and tore their shirts and dresses, that the whole world should make an adjustment. Wasn't that a bit grandiose?

Here, Ellis is calling into question the rationality of the attitude that Lucy attributes to the bereaved parents' group. This is a departure from the standard REBT approach which would encourage Lucy to assume temporarily

that this was normal behaviour and, that she was failing to be normal in this respect. Without having access to Ellis's clinical thinking at that time it is difficult for me to speculate accurately on the reason behind his clinical strategy here. My guess is that Ellis wants Lucy to see the irrationality of that group's attitude so that she stops comparing herself to them.

Lucy: I thought so.

Ellis: And wasn't the group encouraging them to do that, to let it all out, to let their feelings out?

Lucy: Yeah. That was why I stopped going to the group after a number of months.

Ellis: Well, I was just gonna say, don't forget that those groups, because they're a certain way, and I'm not sure about your group, but it sounds like one of these really expressive groups, they have a selective group that keeps going to them. But people like you, you dropped out and you were comparing yourself to those who stayed and you were saying 'I'm abnormal compared to them'.

Lucy: M'mm.

Ellis: Meaning unusual.

Lucy: Yeah. That's exactly it.

Ellis: But let's suppose you are. Why is that bad? That you're not as disorganised and rending your shirt and tearing your hair as much as they? Why is that a bad kind of reaction?

This is another departure from the standard REBT line. Adopting this line Ellis would have said something like: 'Let's suppose you are not normal in your grieving. Why do you *have to* be normal in this respect?' Instead, Ellis is questioning the badness of what he considers an unhealthy reaction for he would, without doubt, consider disorganisation and rending hair and clothing an unhealthy response.

Lucy: Well I don't know. But the thing is that I remember that when she was little I used to sometimes have these nightmares that something awful happened to her and it would be so hideous and I would wake up and realise that it had been a dream and it was such an incredible relief. And here the nightmare became a reality [*Ellis*: Yeah] and I thought how can I deal with this? How is it possible?

Ellis: But you did deal with this.

Lucy: In my own way, I guess.

Ellis: And isn't that very common among us humans? That we think the worst thing that would happen and we think of ourselves as unable to deal with it?

Lucy: Yes.

Ellis: But when an accident happens and we almost get into one or there is a crisis, we almost do deal with it much better than we imagined at the worst. Isn't that a very common trait?

Once again Ellis is normalising Lucy's experience by showing her that humans frequently think that they cannot deal with some kind of tragedy but when it does happen they deal with it. Ellis continues to eschew the standard REBT line and continues his normalisation of Lucy's experience. He would call this general or inelegant REBT, helping a client but not at the level of irrational beliefs (see Ellis, 1979).

Lucy: Well, I suppose it is.

Ellis: And I don't think you're accepting this fact, that most people, after two years, do adjust to the death of their daughter, no matter how shocked they are and they go on with their lives.

More normalisation from Ellis.

Lucy: Well you know, the thing is that this pattern began way before the two years…[*Ellis*: Right] I was going about my business almost two weeks later. Umm, I couldn't deal with certain things, I just could not bring myself to do for a few weeks, I could not go to the supermarket. I just didn't wanna see anybody and deal with that. But shortly after that, I did. I forced myself.

Ellis: And you know why that was good, that you forced yourself to do that?

Lucy: Umm, it was a matter of emotional survival, I think.

Ellis: That's right, emotional survival not only practical survival because you had better do some of those things. You still were a mother, you still were a wife, and therefore you'd better do them. But also when we distract ourselves into any concerted activity, anything that really preoccupies us, then temporarily, not permanently, we forget about the horrors of life and the things that have happened to us and we're able to control our own feelings and be much more accepting of reality. Now if you had the time and you didn't do anything with it and you mainly kept thinking and thinking about the death of your daughter, the death of your daughter, and how awful that was, you would have been much more shattered and much less effective. So that wasn't a bad thing to do, to become preoccupied and force yourself even uncomfortably to do things. We often give that homework assignment in therapy to people, to force themselves to do something that's uncomfortable and then it becomes easier to do it. And you did that kind of thing for a while and I think it was a very good thing even though your group probably didn't approve of it, did they?

Here Ellis does more than normalise Lucy's experience. He is showing her that her responses were healthy, although her bereaved parents' group would not think so. It is emerging that Ellis is trying to offer a powerful alternative view on what constitutes coping in bereavement to

that offered by this group. My guess is that Ellis considers that Lucy has been overly influenced by her eight-month participation in this group.

Lucy: Well, they didn't express it as approval, really, they would say things like well, you know, whatever's your way is fine, it's your way and we all have our own way. It's the feeling that I got, though, that my way did not seem to be the predominant way [*laughing a little*] and that way just didn't feel right for me.

Lucy makes clear that she picked up on the norms of the group and was overly influenced by them.

Ellis: Well, but that's ironic what you're saying because it was your way. It probably was right for you but not [*Lucy*: But not, yeah] for them. Now you seem to feel uncomfortable that you're in a minority.
Lucy: I was, yeah. I was, yes.
Ellis: And that's good, right? Now why is it so bad, to be in a minority and do things your way, grieve in your way, rather than their way. What's so unusual or abnormal about that?

Ellis continues to validate Lucy's experience.

Lucy: Well you see, that is the basic problem that I have had. I've been in therapy for two years and I think it's on the way out but I've always had this problem whereby others' wishes, others' feelings seem to take predominance over mine.
Ellis: Because, if I do my things my way and put my wishes and feelings first, what are you concluding – that's so bad?
Lucy: Well, the…the deviation must be wrong. Something like that.
Ellis: And that makes me what kind of a person if I deviate and I'm wrong?
Lucy: Oh – a bad person.

Lucy reveals her basic problem that she believes she must not deviate from the norm and she is a bad person if she does. She brought this belief to her experience of the bereaved parents' group and concluded that she was bad for not reacting according to the norms of the group. Interestingly, Ellis might have got to this earlier if he had used standard REBT and not spent so much time normalising and validating Lucy's experience!

Ellis: Now how does that follow? Let's just assume for the sake of discussion that you're not only unusual in some trait such as grieving for your daughter but abnormal, really pathological and deliberately assume the worst that that is so. I don't think that was so. I think you reacted in a quite healthy though unusual manner.

But let's suppose you were wrong and pathological. How would that behaviour, that wrongness, make you a bad person?

I am not sure Ellis is quite accurate in his assessment of Lucy's problem here. His ABC of her problem is:

A = I am wrong and pathological in my behaviour
B = I am a bad person for acting badly
C = Not specified, probably guilt

Mine would be:

A = I have deviated from the norms of the group and am abnormal in my behaviour
B = I am a bad person for deviating and for acting abnormally
C = Probably guilt

Lucy: Well, sensibly speaking, it wouldn't [*laughing*].
Ellis: But in your head?
Lucy: Emotionally, I guess, I, you know, I felt that if I did not jive with the others, that there was something wrong with me.

Lucy is supporting my assessment more than Ellis's here. Both she and Ellis are alluding to the insight problem discussed in Chapter 1.

Ellis: Because I *should* be and do what? What's your demand on yourself?
Lucy: Like everybody else. Quote, 'normal'. Whatever.
Ellis: Well, let us even suppose it would be desirable – which I don't happen to agree with – you being like everybody else because then you'd just be like them, you wouldn't be you, but let's suppose it were desirable. Why do you *have* to act desirably?

Ellis is back to the standard REBT approach but, in an aside, is still casting doubt on the wisdom of Lucy's desire to be like everyone else.

Lucy: Ah, well, that dates back to the way I was brought up [*laughing*]. Umm, I now realise that why should I give a shit, you know, it took me a long time, my family…
Ellis: But now wait a minute. It wasn't the way you were brought up, that's a false perception. A lot of people, especially psychoanalysts believe that, that the way you were brought up you adopt, and therefore you make it your own. [*Lucy:* Mm-hmm] But we know if a hundred or a thousand children were brought up exactly the same way as you, they wouldn't be as great conformists all the same as you. Isn't that true? [*Lucy:* Uh-huh] Now, therefore, what

was there about you to begin with that made you listen so carefully to your mother?

As we have seen in his interview with Linda, Ellis casts doubt on the social learning explanation that Lucy gives for her demand.

Lucy: I was always very passive. [*Ellis*: Ahh!] And in my marriage I was. My husband took over and I absorbed his opinions about things.

Ellis: Because if I refuse to go along with people and have their approval, what does that mean about me as a person?

Lucy: Oh, as a person, I'm not sure about that, but I know that it was always caught up in my mind with having to suffer some sort of punishment.

Ellis: I deserve punishment if I do the unusual wrong thing and they don't approve of it, is that right?

Lucy: Right.

Ellis: So, can you see that this was the philosophy which you had as a young child, which was native to you, natural to you, that you brought to the original situation, and that you're bringing now?

Ellis continues to debunk the social learning view and shows Lucy that her philosophy of herself as deserving punishment was natural to her and that she brought this philosophy to her experiences rather than learning it from her experiences. I have seen and heard very many of Ellis's demonstration sessions and he almost always debunks the social learning explanation whenever clients put it forward.

Lucy: Yeah.

Ellis: To this situation. The philosophy that I come second [*Lucy*: Yeah] and other people's approval comes first. [*Lucy*: Yeah] Now let's question that. Why do you have to be second to other people's approval and why must you win their love and acceptance?

Ellis is well and truly back to his usual REBT line here.

Lucy: Well, here again, it's difficult because I no longer feel that I do. I feel that I'm coming out of that now but it was a way of creating a peaceful, no-waves type of picture.

Ellis: Which I had to have?

Lucy: Yes.

Ellis: You see you put in the *had to have* there. But I think you are coming out of it. You sound much better than you were, certainly as a child [*Lucy*: Yeah] and as a young wife and even two years ago but how could you really, solidly get on to it because at times you sink back. You say I'm not mourning, I'm not grieving the way others do, there must be something wrong with me, you feel guilty. Now how can you solidly accept you even if you were quite unusual and not doing what the normal or average person does?

Ellis acknowledges that Lucy has made progress on this 'having to be normal' issue, but notes that she still goes back to it and brings her back to what she first brought up in the interview: her need to grieve in the normal way, i.e. as most others do.

Lucy: Well, I could simply tell myself that there's no question that I am grieving for her [*Ellis*: Right], it may not be the way that someone else might.
Ellis: Right.
Lucy: But I, there's no question that I am.

Lucy doesn't answer Ellis's question.

Ellis: And I'm entitled to what? What are you entitled to?

Ellis notes that Lucy hasn't responded to his question concerning how she could accept herself for her 'abnormal' behaviour and instead switches to undercut her implicit demand: 'I am not entitled to do things my own way when these are against the norm.'

Lucy: Well, to do, to deal with it in my own way. However that way may be.
Ellis: And however people think of me for having my own way. You see? Now if you would really go over that every time you feel guilty or depressed, not grieving and sad about your daughter, because from time to time for the rest of your life you're going to remember this, or read about another accident or something like that, or you'll meet one of her friends, and you'll feel very sad because you believe correctly isn't it most unfortunate that I lost my daughter who was so alive [*Lucy*: Mm-hmm], so good in her way, and now she doesn't exist so you'll feel sad, but we don't want you to feel guilty or depressed because depression usually means: 'The sadness should not, *must* not exist and I can't bear it', and you've shown that you can bear it in fact you've borne it remarkably well and when you don't get guilty about your reactions then you do fine in spite of this real tragedy with your daughter.

Ellis encourages Lucy to go over the idea that she is entitled to her own individual reactions and she does not have to depreciate herself for these when they are against the norm even if others think badly of her for so doing. As is typical of Ellis in demonstration sessions, he does not give her concrete guidance concerning how she can do this. Note also that Ellis is still normalising and validating Lucy's experience of grief while he is doing this.

Lucy: You know, there was, there's something else that happened as a result of what happened to my daughter. And all these things have happened over the past two years. Umm, my way of dealing with what happened to my daughter affected my marriage. [*Ellis*: Right] Right now I'm separated. What happened was that, er, I just could not seem to reach out to my husband in the way that he seemed to need. I was just caught up in my own, holding myself together. [*Ellis*: Right] And so what eventually happened was that he started to have an affair with his 23-year-old secretary, which I learned about last January, which absolutely blew me apart...

Ellis: Which *you* blew you apart because *you* took it too seriously. What did you tell yourself when he had that affair?

Note how Ellis changes Lucy's language from 'which...blew me apart' to 'which *you* blew *you* apart'. In this way, Ellis is implicitly teaching Lucy that she is largely responsible for her feelings because of the beliefs that she holds about events.

Lucy: Well, what it told me was that he was a shit. Really, that was how I felt. I felt that, and I know this sounds like self-pity but I just felt like a dying horse who he had to supply the last few kicks to, to finish the job.

Ellis: So you were saying, how could he do that to me?

Lucy: Yes.

Ellis: In my hour of need.

Lucy: Right.

Ellis: So that is what you told yourself and you felt self-pity and anger at him as a result.

Ellis is using this past ABC, as it were, to teach what we call the iB–C connection, that Lucy's feelings of self-pity and anger were underpinned by the irrational belief ('My husband absolutely should not have treated me in that way') expressed in the rhetorical question, 'How could he do that to me?'

Lucy: Extreme anger. And in that case I didn't seem to have any trouble expressing my feelings, er, of course his response was look, you know, after Sarah died, I just didn't know where to turn and she was there and she comforted me and one thing led to another, you know that whole thing. And that was his view of the situation, in fact right now he claims to have terminated it and, er, he wants to come home.

Ellis: Right.

Lucy: Umm.

Ellis: And how do you feel about that?

Lucy: I feel that all of my anger and hurt and resentment have not really been acknowledged by him. He hasn't really made me feel that I have a right to those feelings. He's tried even to make me assume partial responsibility for this affair.

Ellis: Well, but isn't that because he is defensive and if he thought you were justifiably angry and hurt then he would put himself down so [Lucy: Yeah] he wanted to think that you were 100 per cent responsible but to a degree you are responsible for your hurt and your anger, you know why that is. You're not responsible for what he did. Your anger comes from you and do you know why it comes from you rather than from what he did?

In this response, Ellis is doing two things. First, he is providing an ABC explanation of Lucy's husband's behaviour. This is something that Ellis often does in his demonstrations. Such explanations say to clients, 'This is a possible reason for the other person's behaviour. If I am right, it does not help you to demand that this person must not behave in the way that he did, since his irrational beliefs lead him to behave that way.' Second, Ellis once again teaches Lucy the ABC model, but in his customary way. Thus, he asserts that Lucy makes herself angry and then asks her to explain why this is so.

Lucy: Well, maybe because I feel that, umm, this is something he did to me.

Lucy does not provide the correct answer…

Ellis: And should not have done to me, especially under those conditions.

…so he provides her with the answer. Because of the pressure of time in a demonstration, Ellis does not persist with Socratic questioning if it does not quickly prove to be effective. He would probably persist longer with it in his regular therapy sessions, when he will probably be seeing his clients for several sessions at least.

Lucy: Yes.
Ellis: But he should have done that to you. You know why he should have done that to you?

Once again Ellis makes a didactic point and follows this up with a Socratic question, asking Lucy to reflect on the reason for his didactically made point. Ellis is questioning Lucy's irrational belief using an empirical dispute.

Lucy: Because he did it [laughing].

Lucy provides the right answer. The word 'should' has several different meanings (Dryden, 1998b). When Lucy says that my husband shouldn't have treated me that way, she is employing the absolute, demanding

'should' which says, in essence: Reality absolutely should not be the way that it is. When Ellis says 'But he should have done that to you', he is employing the empirical 'should' which says, in essence: Reality should be the way that it is.

Ellis: That's right. That's his nature.

Lucy: [*laughing*] Yeah.

Ellis: You see, now if you fully accept that, and we're not apologising for him or condoning what he did, especially when he tried to blame you for everything. But if that's his nature, that's his nature and that what he did isn't totally him, yeah? [*Lucy*: Mm-hmm] He has lots of other traits so if you would accept him, but not what he did then you would feel sorry and displeased with his behaviour but you would lose the anger at him. You see if you could fully accept him as a fallible human who did the wrong thing and tried to put everything on you and that's very wrong but he is a person who did a bad thing rather than a bad person, then again you wouldn't feel angry. You see that that's correct?

In this response, Ellis first stresses that Lucy can accept the reality of her husband's behaviour without condemning him. Note how he emphasises in making this point that he isn't condoning her husband's behaviour. Second, Ellis offers Lucy hope in stating that if she really adheres to her rational belief then she will experience healthy negative emotions, i.e. sadness or displeasure. Due to the constraints of a single demonstration session, Ellis does not spend much time on helping Lucy to really accept her rational beliefs, but he does convey the view that Lucy *can* do this and by his disputing interventions is providing Lucy with a model of how she can question her own irrational beliefs.

Lucy: Well, I do, and I would have been able to somehow transcend that business if he had put a clean end to it, when he said he was going to which was about seven months ago, she works for him. [*Ellis*: Yeah] And he had said well listen, I'm going to end it and she'll be leaving the office in a few weeks, just give me some time. Well, weeks went and months went. Now she's leaving, presumably in two weeks. Now during the seven months while we were living apart and I was giving him time and we were continuing to see each other because he wanted to come and visit our daughter and all that, and also I could feel the hurt and rage and resentment just building and building, and I was saying to myself well, it's been seven months, you know, when? And...and he would say things like, I'm dealing with it my own way and when I am ready, she will go, as though I didn't matter, you know?

Ellis: Right, and I hear you saying (1) he took too long and (2) he didn't let me matter and he *should* not, *must* not act that way. Is that right?

This is typical Ellis. He condenses Lucy's experience into its 'A' components (see points 1 and 2 above) and its 'B' component (her demand about her husband's behaviour).

Lucy: Yes.
Ellis: And again, shouldn't he act the way he indubitably does?

Another empirical dispute of Lucy's demand.

Lucy: Well, apparently there was no other way that he did act.
Ellis: Right. And if you would accept him with that bad behaviour and I'm again not apologising for his behaviour or saying that it's good but presume he promised you and then didn't go through with his promises. That's bad behaviour. He was not trustworthy.
Lucy: That is the key. Yeah.
Ellis: But he is a human with untrustworthy behaviour, he's not a lousy, totally untrustworthy human. Do you see the difference?

Ellis now switches to Lucy's other-depreciation belief. In his customary way, he asserts that her irrational belief is false and the rational alternative other-acceptance belief is true and asks her to reflect actively on the difference.

Lucy: Yes, but then, can you have a relationship with someone who you feel is untrustworthy?

Notice how Lucy sidesteps Ellis's question about her beliefs and goes to the issue of whether or not she can live with her husband.

Ellis: If you were un-angry you would decide that. [*Lucy*: Mm-hmm] If you got rid of your anger and your hurt, your self-pity, then you would decide whether it's worth it and that's what we'd better finally decide in life, seeing that a human acts a bad way in our eyes, we don't like it, the way he acts, now does he have another, other compensatory trait?

Ellis reacts to Lucy's sidestep in an interesting way. He shows her that the best time to decide whether or not she wants a relationship with her husband is after she has dealt with her feelings of anger and hurt. By asking if her husband has a compensatory trait, Ellis is leading Lucy back to the issue of other-depreciation and other-acceptance.

Lucy: Oh yeah. Sure, he has many.
Ellis: All right. Now if you are un-angry but still displeased with that particular behaviour and still not trusting him totally, because you didn't trust him and you couldn't trust him in that respect and you would finally decide whether it was worth it.

Ellis reiterates his previous point.

Lucy: Hmmm.
Ellis: So the problem from an emotional standpoint, from a Rational Emotive Behaviour Therapy standpoint, is first to get rid of your self-blaming about your husband and especially about your child, that you contributed to her going away, to accept you totally, even though you may have done the unwise thing in letting her go because you could've stopped her, but don't forget that could have had hassles and problems too because then she would have been upset about being stopped.

At first, Ellis yet again makes the point that Lucy is best advised to deal with her emotional problems before making important life decisions. Then he gets caught up in his own aside and the response peters out and the first point loses its impact.

Lucy: Yeah.
Ellis: But let's just suppose the worst and you did the wrong thing. You are a human who made an error but by the same token your husband, under great duress, under great stress because he was very upset about the child, he had this affair, he lied to you. He prolonged it way beyond what he could've, therefore he is a human who did the wrong thing, but he is not a rotten human. No human is rotten, you know why no human is a rotten person?

Ellis is probably aware that the session will soon be coming to an end, so he links Lucy's problem with self-blame with her problem with blaming her husband, makes the relevant point that no human is rotten and then in his usual fashion asks Lucy to explain the reasoning behind this assertion. Also, note that Ellis here could have stated the more specific point: 'Neither you nor your husband is rotten', but chooses the more general point. Ellis's view is that if you don't try to teach clients a general rational philosophy, they will not learn it. But how many clients will *meaningfully* learn this faithfully in a one-off demonstration session?

Lucy: I don't know if I agree [*laughing*].
Ellis: Why?
Lucy: Umm...
Ellis: Because?
Lucy: You're naming the behaviour and attributing it to the person.

Although Lucy initially does not agree with Ellis's general point about human worth, in response to his request to justify her position, she gives a reason which supports the position that Ellis originally asserted.

Ellis: And we're saying the person is responsible for the behaviour so we're not saying you're not responsible for what you did or that your husband isn't responsible for what he did. But we're saying that a human has so many behaviours, hundreds, thousands in his or her lifetime, that the behaviours change, the human as a whole changes, and too bad, that's the way all humans are, fallible, screwed up, and we don't have to be with them but we'd better first accept ourselves and then, and then later decide whether it's worth it, whether they have so many poor behaviours [*Lucy*: Yeah] that being with them isn't worth it. Now, if you would do that, first totally accept you and then totally accept your husband, but not the way he acts, I'm not saying that, then you can make your own hedonic calculus to see whether it's more pleasurable being with him than not, and then you'll finally decide and if you stay with him fine and if you don't that's OK too, if you see what I mean. [*Lucy*: Yeah] So I want you to give that some thought. Your home-work assignment will be to see that you create your own hurt and your own guilt especially about your daughter, and you can always give that up by totally accepting you. And your husband. He does his bad things but you make yourself angry at him and then you don't know what to do. So that you can de-anger, get rid of your anger at him then decide later what to do. Now if you would work on that then you won't easily make a decision, it'll still be difficult to make a decision, but you will go about your life and be able to make a decision easier. [*Lucy*: Hm-hmm] So if you wanna try what we've been talking about...

There is a lot of information presented in this summary response, perhaps too much. But since everything has been covered in the session, Lucy may be processing what Ellis is summarising. Note how Ellis unilaterally gives Lucy a homework assignment of his choosing without any negotiation. This would not be good practice in regular therapy, but does reflect the stance that Ellis takes in his demonstration sessions, that of authoritative expert.

Ellis makes one mistake where he talks to Lucy about totally accepting herself and her husband. Total acceptance, in this context, is unrealistic and perfectionistic. Still, this mistake does prove that even Ellis isn't perfect!!

Lucy: Yeah.
Ellis: OK. It was certainly good talking with you.
Lucy: It was good talking to you too. Thank you.

8

Ellis's Interview with Peter

Ellis: What problem would you like to start with, Peter?

Peter: Well, I've been avoiding taking responsibility for myself finan-cially, and, umm, I'm back home now.

Ellis: You're living with your parents?

Peter: Yeah.

Ellis: How old are you now?

Peter: Twenty-three.

Ellis: Right. And do you work?

Peter: No. I got back from Sweden and, er, looked at…I'm not motivated to, er, to seek work or anything like that.

Ellis: And how long have you been back?

Peter: About six months.

Ellis: And what did you prepare for doing when you were in Sweden?

Peter: Huh, well, I don't know. I had some vague ideas such as, umm, music, and er, I did a little bit of modelling there.

Ellis: And the only thing you've ever prepared for in life in a sense is modelling. What are you capable of doing if you wanted to do it?

Peter: I think music, and, er…

Ellis: You mean play in a band? Or what?

Peter: Yes. And record also.

Ellis: Yup. And record music, right. As part of a group?

Peter: Yes, and er…

Ellis: And what stops you then from pushing yourself to try to get in a group and play and record music? What stops you from doing that?

Peter: Umm, I hate to say it but I guess a fear of failure.

Ellis: That you won't get in a group or you'll get in one and then fail, or both?

Peter: Yup. The latter. That I'll fail.

Ellis: And they'll see that you're not a great musician?

Peter: Er, yeah, and that my options are slowly, er, receding, you know, or rather, they're getting smaller and smaller.

Ellis: Well you've got them to zero right now [*Peter*: Yes] because you're not doing anything. So even if you did try to get into music and you failed, you still would have other options; but what are you really afraid of, you said fear of failure, now what does that mean to you? If I joined a group and if I wasn't good enough to stay with them and they got rid of me, what, how would you feel at that point?

Peter: I'd say pretty, er, down.

Ellis: Right, do you mean depressed, or, self-downing?

Peter: Yeah. Demoralised.

Ellis: Demoralised. All right. Now at A, the activating event, in the ABC of REBT, you would be failing and at C, the consequence, you would be demoralised and depressed. Now what is B, your belief system, that would make you demoralise yourself?

Peter: Er, well, that I should be able to succeed.

Ellis: Right. That's right on the head. Now, D, disputing why *must* you, *should* you be able to succeed?

Peter: Yeah. Right, you know, I had disputed and, umm, I don't know if it's enough, umm...

Ellis: Well, give the answer. Dispute the 'should'. 'I *should* be able to succeed.' Now when you do that, what's the answer when you say why *must* I, why *should* I succeed, what answer do you give yourself?

Peter: Well that if I don't succeed er, it would be very impractical.

Ellis: Right. But that doesn't answer your question.

Peter: No.

Ellis: No, because you're answering a different question. You see whenever I ask people why must you do this or should you do that, they say as you're saying, because it would be preferable, practical if I did, but why *must* you do what would be preferable, you see? You see you're not really answering me. Now why *must* you do what would be practical or preferable?

Peter: There is no reason why I should be practical, but...

Ellis: But?

Peter: But, this would be preferable.

Ellis: Therefore. I'd better do what?

Peter: Start moving.

Ellis: Move my arse. Right. You see. If there's no reason why I have to, if you really believe that, and I think you very lightly believe that and you're going back to I should, I should, I should [*Peter*: Yeah] and it would be preferable for five or ten reasons that you can give, then what would stop you from pushing yourself and trying especially to get into a group and to play music? What would stop you? If you really did believe it only would be preferable, but I don't have to?

Peter: It's hard to get over that, umm, that have to, umm, I rely on it.

Ellis: Yeah, you see that's right, it's very hard to get over that 'have to' because, you know where you originally got it from, do you know where it stems from that 'have to', 'I *have to* succeed'?

Peter: Well, umm, that my self-esteem relies on my success?

Ellis: Well, that's true, you're saying I *have to* succeed because if I don't I am no good, my self-esteem. But why do people think that way? You're a bright individual and you see, on a certain level that you don't 'have to', there's no reason, yet you go back to that '*have to*', now why is that so strong, that '*have to*'?

Peter: Well, I can cite cultural things like that.

Ellis: No. You can't. Because your culture tells you it's very preferable to.

Peter: Oh!

Ellis: So for example, in some other cultures, if you were in Africa you wouldn't be playing your kind of music but in this culture your culture says that it's very preferable to make a living, to work at something such as music and particularly music since you like it and you're prepared for it. So your culture says it's very preferable but where did you get the '*have to*', I '*have to*' do what's preferable? Now where did that come from?

Peter: That's my own.

Ellis: That's right, you see, you're born as almost all humans are, with a tendency, a very strong tendency to transform preferences into have to's.

Peter: Yeah.

Ellis: And almost all of us do it, especially about *very* important things like working which is very important, or playing music which is very important. So you're saying *because* it's so important, therefore I *have* to and you don't realise when you say that, that that doesn't follow. Do you see that that doesn't follow?

Peter: Yeah.

Ellis: That no matter how important or how preferable it is – and we don't want you to give up your preferences or your values.

Peter: But I still stupidly transform it to...

Ellis: To a '*have to*', yeah. Because that's your nature, you see. And then when you find that you stupidly, as you just said rightly, transform it to a '*have to*', and you *feel* upset, how do you feel about your upsetness, about your despair, your depression?

Peter: Well, that I shouldn't really have it.

Ellis: That's right. You see, now you've got another 'have to'. You start with the first 'have to', I have to do well, then you see that you're not doing well and you make yourself depressed and despairing, then you say oh my God I made myself this, because you know to some degree you don't have to be depressed, not everybody in your position is, and then you say I shouldn't make myself depressed, I shouldn't make myself disorganised. How terrible, and you put you down for the second time, you see. Now if we can get you to stop putting yourself down and stop saying I have to not be depressed and to say I am depressed that's too bad, and then go back to the original I would like very much to succeed in music but I never *have to*, now how can I get what I like? and you'll do music, and music, and music and you probably will get somewhere but if you don't then there's always something else, right?

Peter: It takes a lot of, er, work.

Ellis: That's right and now we come to the second part which we call LFT [low frustration tolerance]. Even when you're upset, right now you could look for a job and one reason you gave which is very important, I don't want to because I might fail. But do you see there's another reason why you don't look for work?

Peter: Yeah, I do, yeah. I also fear being demoralised or depressed about *not* succeeding.

Ellis: Because, if I did a lot of effort and still didn't get the work, what would you then tell yourself about all that effort?

Peter: That it was wasted. I mean, er...

Ellis: And isn't it *terr...ib...le* that I can't get what I want, when I do some work for it? The world should be arranged so that at least if I work I should have a guarantee that I will get what I want, isn't it something like that?

Peter: Yeah.

Ellis: Right. Why must conditions exist so that even if you work, you have a guarantee that you get what you want?

Peter: But that too would be preferable...

Ellis: [*laughing a little*] That's right, but...

Peter: But it doesn't work that way.

Ellis: The conditions don't give a damn for any of us. And right now you said right at the beginning of this session and I think correctly, that work isn't easily available.

Peter: Yeah.

Ellis: Five years ago maybe it would have been, but right now in our economic period and the way music is [*Peter*: Yes], it's not that easily available [*Peter*: No]. So it's very hard going after what you want. Right?

Peter: Yeah.

Ellis: But you are saying it's *too* hard, it shouldn't *be* that hard, when you don't look.

Peter: Well, are you saying that I have no, er, empirical way of saying whether it is too hard or not?

Ellis: *Too* hard is a magical term. *It's* hard is an empirical term. That's describing reality, because if anybody including you looks for work in a field where work is sparse, then you can look and look and look and you might not find anything, so we can prove empirically that it's hard. But you're saying it's *too* hard. Now do you see that that's not an empirical statement, that's a magical statement?

Peter: But, if I work and work and work but never succeed...?

Ellis: Yeah.

Peter: Wouldn't that then be too...?

Ellis: Then it would mean that it would require too much effort and it's not worth it.

Peter: Uh-huh.

Ellis: But you could only prove that by working hard and hard and seeing whether it's worth it. But there's another sense in which you're saying it's 'too hard' and that's the should before. It's *too* hard because it *shouldn't* be as hard as it is. [*Peter:* Yeah] That's low frustration tolerance. Life should be *easier* because I want it to be. Music should be more available to me because I'd enjoy it and like it and make money out of it, you see?

Peter: That sounds a little like my reasoning.

Ellis: That's right. But *should, must* life be easier the way you really would want it?

Peter: Well again it would be preferable but...what do I say?

Ellis: It would be preferable, but...Right.

Peter: It's not that way.

Ellis: That's right. And therefore since I'm not going to get my preference, what?

Peter: Umm. I don't know. I...

Ellis: Or I'm not going to get it easily, because we don't know that you won't get it.

Peter: [*tentatively*] Accept it.

Ellis: Accept the fact that it's hard.

Peter: Yeah.

Ellis: And do what? If you really accept the fact that it's hard, but that's the way it is.

Peter: Whether it's er, practical for me to seek it?

Ellis: Right. Take a certain amount of time, not for ever, really trying every possible door to open to get into music, seeing whether there's a possibility that you would get it, and if you really discovered that you couldn't get into music, I'm not sure that would ever occur but let's suppose it took a year and you're not making it at all, then what could you decide if that were true?

Peter: Umm. Another bleak thing, er, seek other work.

Ellis: That's right, which would be hard but probably har*der* if you don't. Because will your parents take care of you for ever? [*Peter:* No] That's a little unlikely. But you would only know that grim choice probably after you really threw yourself, and threw yourself, and threw yourself for a reasonable length of time, into the music.

Peter: But how would I stop myself from getting, umm, depressed from the fact that I work and work and don't get er, the chances?

Ellis: You mean let's suppose that at what we call A, activating event, you're really pushing your ass to find a job and you're not getting any offers or anything like that and at C, consequence, in your gut, you're feeling depressed because what are you saying about the fact that you're not getting a job which is depressing you? What are you saying to yourself?

Peter: Again, that I should be getting this job?

Ellis: That's right. It shouldn't be that hard. Because I'm trying to get it I *should* be able to get it and isn't it *terrible* and awful that I'm not. Now what's wrong with that statement, that 'it shouldn't be that hard'?

Peter: But that again comes from me. It's not...

Ellis: Right. But why is it wrong? Why is it a foolish statement, that 'it shouldn't be as hard as it is'?

Peter: I think that it's not realistic.

Ellis: Because it is as hard as it is, you see. Now what could you replace it with if you were to imagine, dream up a different statement that would still keep the hardness of it but get rid of your depression what would that new statement be? You'd start off with, 'Yes it's very hard and maybe impossible for me to get a job,' but what?

Peter: Umm. It might be worth it for me to, to er, seek it for a certain amount of time.

Ellis: Right. And if that time passes and I still can't get a job, what?

Peter: Er, lighten up, er, on that desire of mine.

Ellis: Not the desire [*Peter*: No?], the should. You see, you could still always for the rest of your life *wish* that you could get a job because you could work for five years at some other job and then an opening might just accidentally come in music and that would be fine, so you don't give up the desire but the *demand*, the *command*, which is I should be able, or conditions should be able to give me a job right now, and what can you say instead of that?

Peter: Hmm. That...there is no reason why I should get it now.

Ellis: Even though it would be highly preferable.

Peter: Yeah.

Ellis: You see? And really get that into you over and over, and one of the techniques we use in REBT is to use these coping or rational statements very forcefully and really say to yourself many times, 'There is *no* reason why I *have* to get a job in music right now even though it's very preferable and even though I will try and try.'

Peter: But wouldn't...

Ellis: Yeah?

Peter: But wouldn't that diminish my desire?

Ellis: Well, I was just going to say and especially do that after you had tried very hard. Suppose you tried for a year [*Peter*: Oh] and couldn't get it? Right now you're right, it would be better to say, 'Goddamnit I am *determined* to get a job and I will *work* my ass off to get one, try all kinds of things and then you could add, *but* if I don't, *too damn bad*. There's no reason why I *have to* get what I'd like very much to get, you see?

Peter: OK.

Ellis: Now let me give you Rational-Emotive Imagery. This is a different way of doing the same thing. It's an emotive, evocative imagery way of doing it. Now close your eyes and imagine, imagine the worst, now that you really try for a full year, close your eyes and imagine that you really try very hard and you don't get a job and it looks like there's none in music at all. Now try to vividly imagine that situation, you tried hard and there's still no job. Now can you right now vividly imagine that? Close your eyes and vividly imagine that happening. People are saying, 'Well, too bad, music is not good and we can't hire you, besides maybe you're not even good enough', but even if you were, there's no jobs available. Now can you vividly imagine that happening? [*Peter*: Yeah] Right. Now how do you honestly feel in your gut as you imagined that?

Peter: ....Mm'mm, frustrated.

Ellis: Close your eyes and keep imagining that. Very frustrated, and is it only frustration? Do you feel anything in addition to the frustration as you vividly imagine those doors that are closed to you?

Peter: I feel kind of down, too.

Ellis: All right. Now get in touch with that downed, and sort of depressed feeling. Make yourself feel as *down* as you can and tell me when you really feel down in your gut about those doors being closed in music.

Peter: ...I feel down.

Ellis: All right. Now keep the same image and change the feeling of *downed* to only disappointment. Make yourself feel keenly disappointed but not down, not depressed and tell me when you are able to, and I know that you're able to just feel disappointed and not depressed. You can change your feeling.

Peter: ...OK.

Ellis: All right. Now open your eyes. How did you change that feeling, what did you do to change the feeling?

Peter: I, er, accepted it. Umm, I realised that things aren't always going the way I want.

Ellis: Right.

Peter: I've got to lump it.

Ellis: Right.

Peter: Er, and even though it would be preferable had I been successful.

Ellis: Right.

Peter: That there's no reason why I should always be successful.

Ellis: That was excellent. Now you see, what you do for the next 30 days, you see this only took five minutes, at least once a day imagine the worst, let yourself feel very down, very depressed, change it to disappointment the way you just did, and then practise the new feeling, disappointed instead of depression, and the ideas, the cognitions, the thoughts that you just said that go with it, and the new behaviour which would be to probably at that time look for something else if that were true. Now will you do that for at least five minutes a day for the next 30 days and practise that?

Peter: Yeah. OK.

Ellis: Right, in case you don't because you didn't sound enthusiastic, what do you like to do that you do almost every day in the week? Some activity you enjoy?

Peter: Well before that though, I don't know if this would be effective again in my case, the feeling of down-ness isn't very easy to get rid of.

Ellis: No, but we're going to get you to only feel disappointed, you're right, you see, you're now thinking about it and feeling down, but if we can get you to really only feel disappointed rather than down to get rid of the down-ness, then you go back to 'Since it would be so disappointing, I'm gonna move my butt to do better, to really try.'

Peter: No, I mean feeling my down-ness and then bringing it back to disappointment.

Ellis: Right. But you're thinking you can't get rid of it but if you really do this then you'll get rid of it, you see, and you'd be prepared for any rejections because you're not gonna get thoroughly rejected for at least a year, but you're gonna get little rejections along the way. Now we want you, when you feel those little rejections, when you get them, to only feel disappointed and then you'll go on. Right now you're gonna feel down and depressed and you'll stop yourself from going on after even a minor disappointment [*Peter*: Right], you see? [*Peter*: Yeah, true] So if you practise this every time you get rejected, automatically you'll go back to the feeling of disappointment. Do you see what I mean?

Peter: You think so?

Ellis: Oh yes, try it. It's an experiment, you have nothing to lose. Now what do you do every day that you like doing, that you would not want to give up? Something you enjoy every day.

Peter: Umm, bike-riding.

Ellis: All right. No bike-riding for the next 30 days till after you do this five minutes at least once a day of Rational-Emotive Imagery, you see. What do you hate to do that you avoid, that is, something you don't like and you avoid?

Peter: Umm, cleaning up my room.

Ellis: All right. For the next 30 days if 12 midnight arrives and you still haven't done the Rational-Emotive Imagery then clean up your room for another hour till 1 a.m. and otherwise you can have as dirty a room as possible, you see? So that will just help you to do it and if you consistently do it as I said, the goal is to make you feel disappointed, sorry when you actually get rejected but not depressed and down, because that will block you as now is happening. You see, you're being blocked now from doing anything because you know you will often get rejected, especially in today's market and therefore you're turning yourself off.

Peter: It's hard to distinguish between down, depression, and, er, frustration.

Ellis: Well, frustration is first, you feel frustration and then you add the downing and the depression. If you only felt frustrated that could be the same thing as disappointment. You can make yourself feel frustrated and not depressed. Depression means I shouldn't be this frustrated, isn't it awful. You see?

Peter: OK.

Ellis: Now if you work along that line and do the disputing as we discussed before: 'Why is it awful when I get rejected?' 'Why must I succeed?' and 'Why must the world give me what I want when I want it?' then you'll see you'll do much better. Now do you want to work on that for at least the next 30 days or so?

Peter: OK.

Ellis: OK. It was certainly good talking with you.

Peter: Thank you.

9

Commentary on Ellis's Interview with Peter

Ellis: What problem would you like to start with, Peter?

Ellis's usual problem-focused beginning.

Peter: Well, I've been avoiding taking responsibility for myself finan-
cially, and, umm, I'm back home now.
Ellis: You're living with your parents?
Peter: Yeah.
Ellis: How old are you now?
Peter: Twenty-three.
Ellis: Right. And do you work?
Peter: No. I got back from Sweden and, er, looked at…I'm not motivated
to, er, to seek work or anything like that.
Ellis: And how long have you been back?
Peter: About six months.
Ellis: And what did you prepare for doing when you were in Sweden?
Peter: Huh, well, I don't know. I had some vague ideas such as, umm,
music, and er, I did a little bit of modelling there.
Ellis: And the only thing you've ever prepared for in life in a sense is
modelling. What are you capable of doing if you wanted to do it?
Peter: I think music, and, er…
Ellis: You mean play in a band? Or what?
Peter: Yes. And record also.
Ellis: Yup. And record music, right. As part of a group?
Peter: Yes, and er…

**Up to now, Ellis has been gathering some background information so
that he can put Peter's problems in some kind of context. Having done
this, in the following intervention he focuses Peter's attention on
blocks to goal achievement. Unusually, however, Ellis does not ask
Peter how he stops himself from pursuing his goals; instead he uses the
more passive 'what stops you?'**

Ellis: And what stops you then from pushing yourself to try to get in a
group and play and record music? What stops you from doing that?
Peter: Umm, I hate to say it but I guess a fear of failure.

Ellis: That you won't get in a group or you'll get in one and then fail, or both?
Peter: Yup. The latter. That I'll fail.
Ellis: And they'll see that you're not a great musician?
Peter: Er, yeah, and that my options are slowly, er, receding, you know, or rather, they're getting smaller and smaller.
Ellis: Well you've got them to zero right now [*Peter*: Yes] because you're not doing anything. So even if you did try to get into music and you failed, you still would have other options; but what are you really afraid of, you said fear of failure, now what does that mean to you? If I joined a group and if I wasn't good enough to stay with them and they got rid of me, what, how would you feel at that point?

Ellis very nicely shows Peter that by doing nothing he is limiting himself far more than he would if he attempted an active pursuit of his musical goals and failed. He then asks for clarification concerning Peter's feelings were he to fail (i.e. the emotional C in the ABC framework).

Peter: I'd say pretty, er, down.
Ellis: Right, do you mean depressed, or, self-downing?
Peter: Yeah. Demoralised.
Ellis: Demoralised. All right. Now at A, the activating event, in the ABC of REBT, you would be failing and at C, the consequence, you would be demoralised and depressed. Now what is B, your belief system, that would make you demoralise yourself?

Ellis very economically teaches Peter the ABC framework by utilising the material he has just obtained from Peter and then goes straight to the assessment of B.

Peter: Er, well, that I should be able to succeed.

Peter's response indicates to me that he is familiar with REBT. Whether Ellis knew this before the interview is not clear.

Ellis: Right. That's right on the head. Now, D, disputing why *must* you, *should* you be able to succeed?

Once again Ellis goes straight to disputing the irrational belief as soon as the volunteer client discloses it.

Peter: Yeah. Right, you know, I had disputed and, umm, I don't know if it's enough, umm…

It is clear now that Peter is familiar with REBT. He claims to have already disputed his irrational belief, but seemingly without much success.

Ellis: Well, give the answer. Dispute the 'should'. 'I *should* be able to succeed.' Now when you do that, what's the answer when you say why *must* I, why *should* I succeed, what answer do you give yourself?

Ellis wants to assess for himself *how* Peter disputes his irrational belief. REBT therapists want to know why clients' disputing fails, and encouraging clients to dispute their irrational beliefs live in the session is an excellent way of gathering important information on this point.

Peter: Well that if I don't succeed er, it would be very impractical.
Ellis: Right. But that doesn't answer your question.

As Peter's response shows, his attempt to dispute his own irrational belief is poor and, as Ellis informs him, he doesn't answer his own disputing question.

Peter: No.
Ellis: No, because you're answering a different question. You see whenever I ask people why must you do this or should you do that, they say as you're saying, because it would be preferable, practical if I did, but why *must* you do what would be preferable, you see? You see you're not really answering me. Now why *must* you do what would be practical or preferable?

As Ellis clearly shows Peter, a common response to an empirical dispute of an irrational demand (e.g. 'I must succeed') is to provide a reason in support of the rational preference ('I want to succeed'). The only correct answer to the question 'Why do I have to succeed?' is 'I don't'.

Peter: There is no reason why I should be practical, but…
Ellis: But?
Peter: But, this would be preferable.
Ellis: Therefore. I'd better do what?

In this brief intervention, Ellis is teaching Peter a very important point: that a rational belief promotes action. This is very important in this session because the content of what Peter is discussing with Ellis and in his behaviour in the session show that one of Peter's major problems is inactivity. By suggesting that Peter ask himself 'Therefore, I'd better do what?', Ellis is stressing the importance of taking action if one wishes to achieve one's goals.

Peter: Start moving.
Ellis: Move my arse. Right. You see. If there's no reason why I have to, if you really believe that, and I think you very lightly believe that and you're going back to I should, I should, I should [*Peter*: Yeah] and it

would be preferable for five or ten reasons that you can give, then what would stop you from pushing yourself and trying especially to get into a group and to play music? What would stop you? If you really did believe it only would be preferable, but I don't have to?

Ellis alerts Peter to the insight problem first discussed in Chapter 1. His problem is that he only has a very lightly held conviction in his rational belief and thus easily goes back to his irrational belief.

Peter: It's hard to get over that, umm, that have to, umm, I rely on it.

Ellis: Yeah, you see that's right, it's very hard to get over that 'have to' because, you know where you originally got it from, do you know where it stems from that 'have to', 'I *have to* succeed'?

Peter: Well, umm, that my self-esteem relies on my success?

Ellis: Well, that's true, you're saying I *have to* succeed because if I don't I am no good, my self-esteem. But why do people think that way? You're a bright individual and you see, on a certain level that you don't 'have to', there's no reason, yet you go back to that '*have to*', now why is that so strong, that 'have to'?

Peter: Well, I can cite cultural things like that.

Ellis: No. You can't. Because your culture tells you it's very preferable to.

Peter: Oh!

Ellis: So for example, in some other cultures, if you were in Africa you wouldn't be playing your kind of music but in this culture your culture says that it's very preferable to make a living, to work at something such as music and particularly music since you like it and you're prepared for it. So your culture says it's very preferable but where did you get the '*have* to', I '*have* to' do what's preferable? Now where did that come from?

Peter: That's my own.

Ellis: That's right, you see, you're born as almost all humans are, with a tendency, a very strong tendency to transform preferences into have to's.

Ellis stresses to Peter that he is the author of his own demandingness. His culture helps to give the content of his preference, but as a human he transforms this preference into a demand because this is what humans tend to do. Ellis creates the opportunity to teach Peter about the prevalence of nature over nurture in creating psychological disturbance. As the interviews in this book show, Ellis does like to get this point over in demonstration sessions as well as in regular therapy sessions. Ellis's argument is that encouraging clients to see that they create their demands rather than that demands are created by culture, society or upbringing, helps them to take responsibility for disputing and changing these irrational beliefs. If this is the case, Ellis needs to make the latter point much more explicit to Peter here and in the following exchanges.

Peter: Yeah.

Ellis: And almost all of us do it, especially about *very* important things like working which is very important, or playing music which is very important. So you're saying *because* it's so important, therefore I *have* to and you don't realise when you say that, that that doesn't follow. Do you see that that doesn't follow?

Here, Ellis uses a logical dispute of a demand.

Peter: Yeah.

In a regular session, Ellis probably wouldn't have taken Peter's 'Yeah' as a sign that he actually understands the illogical nature of creating a demand from a preference. This is, another instance of the difference between a one-off demonstration session where time is of the essence and regular therapy, where Ellis would have engaged Peter in more of a dialogue on this point.

Ellis: That no matter how important or how preferable it is and we don't want you to give up your preferences or your values.

Again this shows Ellis stressing to clients when he is encouraging them to dispute their demands that he does not want them to give up their preferences.

Peter: But I still stupidly transform it to…

Ellis: To a *'have to'*, yeah. Because that's your nature, you see. And then when you find that you stupidly, as you just said rightly, transform it to a *'have to'*, and you *feel* upset, how do you feel about your upsetness, about your despair, your depression?

Here Ellis is assessing for the presence of a meta-emotional problem.

Peter: Well, that I shouldn't really have it.

Ellis: That's right. You see, now you've got another 'have to'. You start with the first 'have to', I have to do well, then you see that you're not doing well and you make yourself depressed and despairing, then you say oh my God I made myself this, because you know to some degree you don't have to be depressed, not everybody in your position is, and then you say I shouldn't make myself depressed, I shouldn't make myself disorganised. How terrible, and you put you down for the second time, you see. Now if we can get you to stop putting yourself down and stop saying I have to not be depressed and to say I am depressed that's too bad, and then go back to the original I would like very much to succeed in music but I never *have to*, now how can I get what I like? and you'll do music, and music, and music and you probably will get somewhere but if you don't then there's always something else, right?

Note that Ellis does not do any work to dispute the irrational beliefs that underpin Peter's meta-emotional problem. Rather he advises Peter that he needs to dispute these beliefs for himself before going back to his original problem. Again, this is probably due to the pressure of time.

Peter: It takes a lot of, er, work.
Ellis: That's right and now we come to the second part which we call LFT [low frustration tolerance]. Even when you're upset, right now you could look for a job and one reason you gave which is very important, I don't want to because I might fail. But do you see there's another reason why you don't look for work?
Peter: Yeah, I do, yeah. I also fear being demoralised or depressed about *not* succeeding.
Ellis: Because, if I did a lot of effort and still didn't get the work, what would you then tell yourself about all that effort?
Peter: That it was wasted. I mean, er...
Ellis: And isn't it *terr...ib...le* that I can't get what I want, when I do some work for it? The world should be arranged so that at least if I work I should have a guarantee that I will get what I want, isn't it something like that?
Peter: Yeah.

In the foregoing interchanges, Ellis directs Peter's attention to the low frustration tolerance beliefs which, given his general level of inactivity, are probably Peter's main problem. In the next response, Ellis disputes the demand implicit in Peter's LFT beliefs.

Ellis: Right. Why must conditions exist so that even if you work, you have a guarantee that you get what you want?
Peter: But that too would be preferable...
Ellis: [*laughing a little*] That's right, but...
Peter: But it doesn't work that way.
Ellis: The conditions don't give a damn for any of us. And right now you said right at the beginning of this session and I think correctly, that work isn't easily available.
Peter: Yeah.
Ellis: Five years ago maybe it would have been, but right now in our economic period and the way music is [*Peter*: Yes], it's not that easily available [*Peter*: No]. So it's very hard going after what you want. Right?
Peter: Yeah.
Ellis: But you are saying it's *too* hard, it shouldn't *be* that hard, when you don't look.

Ellis shows Peter another variant of his LFT philosophy, that he is jumping from 'It is hard in the present climate to pursue a career in music' to 'It is *too* hard to do so'.

Peter: Well, are you saying that I have no, er, empirical way of saying whether it is too hard or not?

Ellis: *Too* hard is a magical term. *It's* hard is an empirical term. That's describing reality, because if anybody including you looks for work in a field where work is sparse, then you can look and look and look and you might not find anything, so we can prove empirically that it's hard. But you're saying it's *too* hard. Now do you see that that's not an empirical statement, that's a magical statement?

Peter: But, if I work and work and work but never succeed…?

Ellis: Yeah.

Peter: Wouldn't that then be too…?

Ellis: Then it would mean that it would require too much effort and it's not worth it.

Peter: Uh-huh.

Ellis: But you could only prove that by working hard and hard and seeing whether it's worth it. But there's another sense in which you're saying it's 'too hard' and that's the should before. It's *too* hard because it *shouldn't* be as hard as it is. [*Peter*: Yeah] That's low frustration tolerance. Life should be *easier* because I want it to be. Music should be more available to me because I'd enjoy it and like it and make money out of it, you see?

Ellis shows Peter quite elegantly that it is only by working hard and evaluating the effects of this hard work that he can determine the wisdom of making further efforts. He then points out the implicit demand that underpins Peter's conclusion that it is is 'too hard' to make these efforts.

Peter: That sounds a little like my reasoning.

Ellis: That's right. But *should*, *must* life be easier the way you really would want it?

Peter: Well again it would be preferable but…what do I say?

Ellis: It would be preferable, but…Right.

Peter: It's not that way.

Ellis: That's right. And therefore since I'm not going to get my preference, what?

Peter: Umm. I don't know. I…

Ellis: Or I'm not going to get it easily, because we don't know that you won't get it.

Peter: [*tentatively*] Accept it.

Ellis: Accept the fact that it's hard.

Peter: Yeah.

Ellis: And do what? If you really accept the fact that it's hard, but that's the way it is.

Peter: Whether it's er, practical for me to seek it?

Ellis: Right. Take a certain amount of time, not for ever, really trying every possible door to open to get into music, seeing whether there's a possibility that you would get it, and if you really discovered that you couldn't get into music, I'm not sure that would ever occur but let's suppose it took a year and you're not making it at all, then what could you decide if that were true?

Once again, Ellis stresses the importance of Peter taking action both to strengthen his rational beliefs and to discover how likely it is that he will succeed musically.

Peter: Umm. Another bleak thing, er, seek other work.

Ellis: That's right, which would be hard but probably har*der* if you don't. Because will your parents take care of you for ever? [*Peter*: No] That's a little unlikely. But you would only know that grim choice probably after you really threw yourself, and threw yourself, and threw yourself for a reasonable length of time, into the music.

Peter: But how would I stop myself from getting, umm, depressed from the fact that I work and work and don't get er, the chances?

Note how Ellis helps Peter by putting his question into the ABC framework. He is modelling this skill for Peter.

Ellis: You mean let's suppose that at what we call A, activating event, you're really pushing your ass to find a job and you're not getting any offers or anything like that and at C, consequence, in your gut, you're feeling depressed because what are you saying about the fact that you're not getting a job which is depressing you? What are you saying to yourself?

Peter: Again, that I should be getting this job?

Ellis: That's right. It shouldn't be that hard. Because I'm trying to get it I *should* be able to get it and isn't it *terrible* and awful that I'm not. Now what's wrong with that statement, that 'it shouldn't be that hard'?

Again Ellis disputes the client's demand as soon as it is expressed.

Peter: But that again comes from me. It's not…

Ellis: Right. But why is it wrong? Why is it a foolish statement, that 'it shouldn't be as hard as it is'?

Peter: I think that it's not realistic.

Ellis: Because it is as hard as it is, you see. Now what could you replace it with if you were to imagine, dream up a different statement that would still keep the hardness of it but get rid of your depression what would that new statement be? You'd start off with, 'Yes it's very hard and maybe impossible for me to get a job,' but what?

There is some evidence here that Ellis is doing too much of the work for Peter. Thus, when Peter replied above that his irrational belief 'it shouldn't be as hard as it is' is unrealistic, Ellis could have asked Peter to explain his answer rather than didactically explaining its lack of realism to Peter. With clients like Peter who have LFT and tend to be laconic, it is important to encourage them to be more active in the session and to do less of the work for them. Ellis does encourage Peter to think for himself to some extent, but not enough in my opinion.

Peter: Umm. It might be worth it for me to, to er, seek it for a certain amount of time.
Ellis: Right. And if that time passes and I still can't get a job, what?
Peter: Er, lighten up, er, on that desire of mine.
Ellis: Not the desire [*Peter*: No?], the should. You see, you could still always for the rest of your life *wish* that you could get a job because you could work for five years at some other job and then an opening might just accidentally come in music and that would be fine, so you don't give up the desire but the *demand*, the *command*, which is I should be able, or conditions should be able to give me a job right now, and what can you say instead of that?

Like many clients, Peter does not clearly see the difference between his desire and his demand. Ellis is very alert to this and uses every opportunity (as here) to teach clients the clear difference between the two.

Peter: Hmm. That…there is no reason why I should get it now.
Ellis: Even though it would be highly preferable.
Peter: Yeah.
Ellis: You see? And really get that into you over and over, and one of the techniques we use in REBT is to use these coping or rational statements very forcefully and really say to yourself many times, 'There is *no* reason why I *have* to get a job in music right now even though it's very preferable and even though I will try and try.'

Ellis suggests the use of *forceful* rational coping statements because he knows that Peter needs to be forceful with himself if he is to stand a chance of convincing himself of his rational beliefs.

Peter: But wouldn't…
Ellis: Yeah?
Peter: But wouldn't that diminish my desire?

Like many clients, Peter thinks that surrendering his demand means weakening his desire. It doesn't, because although what I call a full preference stresses that you don't have to get what you want, it also emphasises that you have desires which of course can be very strong. Ellis tackles this issue in a slightly different way, as shown below.

Ellis: Well, I was just going to say and especially do that after you had tried very hard. Suppose you tried for a year [*Peter*: Oh] and couldn't get it? Right now you're right, it would be better to say, 'Goddamnit I am *determined* to get a job and I will *work* my ass off to get one, try all kinds of things and then you could add, *but* if I don't, *too damn bad*. There's no reason why I *have to* get what I'd like very much to get, you see?
Peter: OK.
Ellis: Now let me give you Rational-Emotive Imagery. This is a different way of doing the same thing. It's an emotive, evocative imagery way of doing it. Now close your eyes and imagine, imagine the worst, now that you really try for a full year, close your eyes and imagine that you really try very hard and you don't get a job and it looks like there's none in music at all. Now try to vividly imagine that situation, you tried hard and there's still no job. Now can you right now vividly imagine that? Close your eyes and vividly imagine that happening. People are saying, 'Well, too bad, music is not good and we can't hire you, besides maybe you're not even good enough', but even if you were, there's no jobs available. Now can you vividly imagine that happening? [*Peter*: Yeah] Right. Now how do you honestly feel in your gut as you imagined that?
Peter: …Mm'mm, frustrated.
Ellis: Close your eyes and keep imagining that. Very frustrated, and is it only frustration? Do you feel anything in addition to the frustration as you vividly imagine those doors that are closed to you?
Peter: I feel kind of down, too.
Ellis: All right. Now get in touch with that downed, and sort of depressed feeling. Make yourself feel as *down* as you can and tell me when you really feel down in your gut about those doors being closed in music.
Peter: …I feel down.
Ellis: All right. Now keep the same image and change the feeling of *downed* to only disappointment. Make yourself feel keenly disappointed but not down, not depressed and tell me when you are able to, and I know that you're able to just feel disappointed and not depressed. You can change your feeling.

Peter: …OK.

Ellis: All right. Now open your eyes. How did you change that feeling, what did you do to change the feeling?

Peter: I, er, accepted it. Umm, I realised that things aren't always going the way I want.

Ellis: Right.

Peter: I've got to lump it.

Ellis: Right.

Peter: Er, and even though it would be preferable had I been successful.

Ellis: Right.

Peter: That there's no reason why I should always be successful.

Ellis: That was excellent. Now you see, what you do for the next 30 days, you see this only took five minutes, at least once a day imagine the worst, let yourself feel very down, very depressed, change it to disappointment the way you just did, and then practise the new feeling, disappointed instead of depression, and the ideas, the cognitions, the thoughts that you just said that go with it, and the new behaviour which would be to probably at that time look for something else if that were true. Now will you do that for at least five minutes a day for the next 30 days and practise that?

Peter: Yeah. OK.

Ellis: Right, in case you don't because you didn't sound enthusiastic, what do you like to do that you do almost every day in the week? Some activity you enjoy?

As discussed in Chapter 1, Ellis often uses Rational-Emotive Imagery as a way of encouraging clients to practise disputing irrational beliefs. Here Ellis's use of REI is typical of the way he generally employs this technique.

Peter: Well before that though, I don't know if this would be effective again in my case, the feeling of down-ness isn't very easy to get rid of.

Peter's response here is another indication of his LFT philosophy. He notes correctly that his feeling of 'down-ness' is not easy to get rid of and thinks that because of this REI would not be effective. My hypothesis is that implicit in this statement is an irrational belief along the lines that 'REI must help me to get rid of my down feeling fairly easily'. Ellis in the exchanges that follow does not intervene at this level.

Ellis: No, but we're going to get you to only feel disappointed, you're right, you see, you're now thinking about it and feeling down, but if we can get you to really only feel disappointed rather than down to get rid of the down-ness, then you go back to 'Since it would be so disappointing, I'm gonna move my butt to do better, to really try.'

Peter: No, I mean feeling my down-ness and then bringing it back to disappointment.

Ellis: Right. But you're thinking you can't get rid of it but if you really do this then you'll get rid of it, you see, and you'd be prepared for any rejections because you're not gonna get thoroughly rejected for at least a year, but you're gonna get little rejections along the way. Now we want you, when you feel those little rejections, when you get them, to only feel disappointed and then you'll go on. Right now you're gonna feel down and depressed and you'll stop yourself from going on after even a minor disappointment [*Peter*: Right], you see? [*Peter*: Yeah, true] So if you practise this every time you get rejected, automatically you'll go back to the feeling of disappointment. Do you see what I mean?

Peter: You think so?

Ellis: Oh yes, try it. It's an experiment, you have nothing to lose. Now what do you do every day that you like doing, that you would not want to give up? Something you enjoy every day.

Peter: Umm, bike-riding.

Ellis: All right. No bike-riding for the next 30 days till after you do this five minutes at least once a day of Rational-Emotive Imagery, you see. What do you hate to do that you avoid, that is, something you don't like and you avoid?

Peter: Umm, cleaning up my room.

Ellis: All right. For the next 30 days if 12 midnight arrives and you still haven't done the Rational-Emotive Imagery then clean up your room for another hour till 1 a.m. and otherwise you can have as dirty a room as possible, you see? So that will just help you to do it and if you consistently do it as I said, the goal is to make you feel disappointed, sorry when you actually get rejected but not depressed and down, because that will block you as now is happening. You see, you're being blocked now from doing anything because you know you will often get rejected, especially in today's market and therefore you're turning yourself off.

Because of Peter's entrenched LFT philosophy and his inactivity, I might have put more emphasis on behavioural ways of acting on his developing rational beliefs rather than on REI, which involves the fairly passive behaviour of sitting and imagining scenarios. Instead, Peter needs to take action in the world with his eyes wide open in ways that strengthen his rational beliefs. I might have suggested some behavioural assignments with the conjoint forceful rehearsal of rational coping statements.

Peter: It's hard to distinguish between down, depression, and, er, frustration.

Ellis: Well, frustration is first, you feel frustration and then you add the downing and the depression. If you only felt frustrated that could be the same thing as disappointment. You can make yourself feel frustrated and not depressed. Depression means I shouldn't be this frustrated, isn't it awful. You see?

Peter: OK.

Ellis: Now if you work along that line and do the disputing as we discussed before: 'Why is it awful when I get rejected?' 'Why must I succeed?' and 'Why must the world give me what I want when I want it?' then you'll see you'll do much better. Now do you want to work on that for at least the next 30 days or so?

Peter: OK.

Ellis: OK. It was certainly good talking with you.

Peter: Thank you.

10

Ellis's Interview with Yvonne

In this chapter, we provide a transcript of a demonstration session conducted by Ellis with a volunteer from the cohort of trainees on an introductory REBT training course. This interview was conducted towards the end of the course, so Yvonne, the trainee, will have learned about the basics of REBT theory and practice and will have had an opportunity to practise REBT in peer counselling sessions. As Yvonne will have been taught the ABCs of REBT, Ellis probably takes this into account and explains less about REBT than he would do if Yvonne knew nothing about this approach to therapy.

The trainees on the programme will have agreed to treat in confidence the material discussed by trainee volunteers and the latter will have given their permission for the interview to be taped for later professional use.

Ellis: OK, what problem would you like to raise?

Yvonne: I'd like to raise something that was raised yesterday, that I thought I had, er, completely overcome.

Ellis: Yeah, what was that?

Yvonne: Well, it was pointed out to me, that I said, er: 'Well I don't torture myself any more.' I mean, that was 20 years ago I tortured myself, no more, and two of the young men in the room said: 'Is that so? Because 20 minutes ago [*laughing*] you know, I heard you torturing yourself.'

Ellis: Yeah.

Yvonne: And I thought, wow, you know. Right, I just do it in smaller bits now. I used to do it globally and, er…

Ellis: And they picked that up that you were still torturing yourself.

Yvonne: Right. And that…er…I was very disappointed.

Ellis: Because you thought that you had ended that sort of thing?

Yvonne: I thought I had conquered that.

Ellis: And they sort of brought to your attention again that you're still torturing yourself. And in what way would you say you're mainly torturing yourself now that you're looking at it?

Yvonne: Well, what brought it up, er…yesterday, was this…this whole practicum. Er…that I'm very…[*sighing*], I'm very disturbed by the fact that I don't think I do it well, that when I do the sessions with one partner that, you know, I just seem to be either floating round in the air or…or blocking, and everybody else seems to be doing so well. And this was the basis of the torture.

Ellis: So, first you *see* that they're doing better than you, you're not doing that well, and then you torture yourself, if I understand you correctly, *about* seeing that. Is that right?

Yvonne: Yes, er…but as you say, first you see I…I realise…something clicks in, and I'm evaluating it that way, I'm perceiving it that way, it doesn't necessarily have to *be* that way.

Ellis: Right. But you could perceive it and evaluate it differently. But first let's assume, because you may be exaggerating, you may not be doing *that* poorly, but let's just assume for the sake of discussion that what you're seeing, your perception, is accurate. You *are* doing poorly. Then, how do you torture yourself about that? What is your evaluation, as you just sort of indicated?

Yvonne: I don't know if I would say that I torture myself. I think I, er more or less begin to say: 'Well this isn't so important anyhow and I guess I really don't wanna do this *really*, it's just taking up a week of time and that's great. It's interesting but, er…you know, it's not that important.'

Ellis: So, we would call that withdrawal. You sort of withdraw from the situation, and view it as not very important, is that right?

Yvonne: Yeah.

Ellis: But do you think that *underneath* that view, that 'I'm finding this not important', you're first sort of torturing yourself and therefore withdrawing. Is that your view of the torture?

Yvonne: I don't know, I'm not really, er…yeah…yeah.

Ellis: Do you think that may be going on?

Yvonne: I'm having a little trouble with defining torture.

Ellis: All right. But we can even skip torture, because we can just look at what we call C, the consequence, which would be withdrawal. So, at A, the activating event in our system of Rational Emotive Behaviour Therapy, you're perceiving that you're not doing well and we're assuming, you and I, that that's true – that may be false, but let's assume that's true – and then at C, you withdraw, maybe defensively. Is that right?

Yvonne: Yes.

Ellis: That maybe you're withdrawing defensively, but at least you withdraw. Now, what do you think you're telling yourself at B, to cause that withdrawal?

Yvonne: OK, umm, 'I'm not as bright as I think I am', er…'these guys are really far more well-trained than…I am', umm, 'They're more perceptive than I am', 'I really have no perception…I don't know what the hell I'm doing', er…'I can't even drag out of a session the kernel of the problem, and if I'm lucky enough to happen on the kernel of the problem, *what do I do*?' You know, er,

I'm er...I don't know what to do, I don't feel schooled, or trained, or...or able, umm, to *be* a therapist.

Ellis: Right. Those are all observations that you're making about your performance compared with their performance. 'I'm not bright enough', 'I'm not well-schooled enough', 'I seem to be confused about what to do'; is that right?

Yvonne: Yes.

Ellis: You're observing those things about your performance compared with *their* performance.

Yvonne: Well, I thought I was feeling those things.

Ellis: Well, but at first; isn't there an observation that that's what you see? We'll get to the feeling in a minute, and we know the behaviour to a certain degree already: you're withdrawing. But once you perceive those things, and let's just assume the worst – we like to assume the worst in REBT just to show people that they can go with even the worst – so, let's assume you're accurate, you're quite accurate, that compared with them you are below par and that as a therapist compared with them again you're not so hot. That's what you're perceiving and evaluating, you're right, you are evaluating that. But *that* kind of observation and evaluation of performance wouldn't make you withdraw. Do you know why it wouldn't make you withdraw if you only stuck with that kind of observation and evaluation: why wouldn't you withdraw?

Yvonne: Possibly because I see others who are equally inept.

Ellis: That would be one thing. That's right. You see others who are inept. But also you could conclude: 'Even though this is so, I'm glad I now see that. Maybe I'd better throw myself into it more and get more training and overcome these deficiencies.' Couldn't that be a legitimate conclusion?

Yvonne: Yes...yes.

Ellis: And then you wouldn't withdraw.

Yvonne: Right.

Ellis: But we know that you *did* feel like withdrawing. Right?

Yvonne: Yes.

Ellis: That's your feeling: 'I don't wanna be here. I'd better withdraw.' Now, therefore, we believe in REBT that there's an additional evaluation. In addition to the evaluation of your performance, you're saying something *stronger* about it and about *you*. Now, if I'm right about that, and I could be wrong but I'm just hypothesising now, what would you be saying that's *stronger* that would make you withdraw?

Yvonne: If I continue I'm gonna make a real ass of myself.

Ellis: And if I make an ass of myself...

Yvonne: If I make a real ass of myself [*laughing*], it's another notch in my belt of asshood.

Ellis: Right. And that proves *what* about you?

Yvonne: That I will die an ass.

Ellis: I will *always* be an ass, I'm a hopeless ass do you mean, or something like that?

Yvonne: I am never going to er…I am never going to get it all straightened out.

Ellis: Right. Now, do you see then, that you have two sets of observations and evaluations? The first one, merely 'Compared with them I'm not doing well, and maybe I never will.' And that *might* be true, you see. It could be that you're just evaluating correctly, that your performance is never going to be up to theirs. But *then* you say: 'My performance makes me an ass and a hopeless ass and I'll *die* an ass as I *live* an ass,' is that right?

Yvonne: Yes.

Ellis: Now *that's* the evaluation…

Yvonne: [*laughing*] My God, that sounds terrible.

Ellis: That's right, you see. And that's what we want to question, and that's why we go to D, disputing. Let's suppose the worst again, that your observation is true and let's even suppose you go *on* acting this way, you're not very good at therapy as they are. How does that make you, a human, an ass?

Yvonne: I guess somewhere I feel that I *have to* excel at *something*.

Ellis: Right. You see the '*have to*'.

Yvonne: I *have to* excel at something.

Ellis: And if you change that '*have to*', to 'I'd *like to* excel at something, but if I don't, I don't', would you then feel like an ass?

Yvonne: No, I wouldn't. But I really have to change the whole statement anyway. I *have to* excel at *everything*. I want to excel at *everything* I touch.

Ellis: Well, but you notice you just said two things. I *want to* excel at everything', which I think almost every human says, 'I'd *like to*', 'I *want to* excel at all *important* things'. Not tiddly-winks, you don't care if you don't excel at tiddly-winks, do you?

Yvonne: No, that would be all right. *That* would show that I was only human.

Ellis: Yes, right. But you want to excel at every important thing and then you say 'and therefore I *have to*', is that right?

Yvonne: Yes.

Ellis: Now, in REBT we never question desires, preferences, wishes, wants, because you could *want* anything. You could want, right now, 10 million dollars, or to be the greatest genius at therapy in the world, and as long as you were saying 'I *want to*, but I don't *have to*', you wouldn't be into trouble. But we question the '*have to*'. Why *must* you excel at an important thing like therapy? Why must you?

Yvonne: I don't know.

Ellis: Well, think about that.

Yvonne: Well, I dunno. I suppose…er…I think it may be that I'm a product of growing up where I've been told, or it's been implied that if you do something, do it well.

Ellis: Right. Let's suppose that's true. And, incidentally, that has sense to it, because if you do something well, it would be *preferable* to doing it poorly. We all learn that because that's not false. Our parents and our schools and our books teach us to try to do well. 'If at once you don't succeed, try try again to succeed.' Isn't that what it means? And so that's OK. But we're still asking another question, not why it's *preferable* to do well, why *must* you do what's preferable? Why do you *have to*?

Yvonne: I feel better when I…when I *do* accomplish. I feel better about myself.

Ellis: Ah, about *yourself*. But you see you've just again said two things, (1) 'I feel better about *it*', which we hope is true – that you would feel better about accomplishment rather than sitting on your rump and doing nothing or doing badly. So you'd better feel better about it. But you're saying 'I feel better about *me*, I only accept *me* when I do *it* well.' Now, is *that* a legitimate conclusion? 'I can only accept *me*, *myself*, my *being*, my *totality* when I do *it*, therapy, well.' Now is that a good conclusion?

Yvonne: You mean, is it accurate?

Ellis: Well, will it give you good results?

Yvonne: No, it won't give me good results.

Ellis: It'll give you what you have…withdrawal, anxiety. Maybe what you said at the beginning of this session, some kind of anguish, terror almost, which may be the thing that is making you withdraw – which we could just guess about, but it certainly *won't give you pleasure* and it won't help you to stay with this practicum or any other thing that you enter. You'll tend to run away. And by running away will you do as well as you'd like to do?

Yvonne: No.

Ellis: You'll normally do worse, isn't that so?

Yvonne: Well, I will not have accomplished anything at all.

Ellis: That's right.

Yvonne: Except to have reinforced again, once again, Yvonne strikes out.

Ellis: That's the irony, you see. That's really an irony. By demanding that 'I must do "X" well', such as therapy in a practicum. 'I *have to*', 'I *have to*', 'I've *got to*', 'I've *got to* do it well', you will withdraw and not even do it *at all*. You see the *need*, the *necessity* of performing well leads to withdrawal or anxiety which interferes with your performance. You see that's catch-22. Now, how do you think you can get out of that bind?

Yvonne: By not withdrawing and not being anxious.

Ellis: That's right. First, not withdrawing. Then you still would be anxious if you didn't withdraw. Now, how could you get rid of your anxiety? Let's assume you stayed with it, and it was *uncomfortable* to stay. And that's what we recommend in REBT, to stay with your discomfort until you make yourself comfortable. How could you get rid of the anxiety by staying with your discomfort?

Yvonne: By applying myself more, and er...learning the techniques.

Ellis: Right. That's one way, but that's a little inelegant. That would work, because let's suppose that you stayed with it no matter how uncomfortable you felt and you learned the techniques of doing therapy. You got better at it and you felt *un-anxious*. Do you *realise* why that would be an inelegant kind of solution? It would work, temporarily, but why would it only work temporarily? Why would it be inelegant?

Yvonne: Because I think it attacks just a very small piece of it.

Ellis: That's right. And even in that small piece, suppose you first did well, and then later did badly. Suppose you finished the practicum, learned REBT quite well, as well as anybody does, and then compare yourself with other therapists and *still* do poorly. Then what would you go back to telling yourself?

Yvonne: That I really don't belong here. I'll go back to the same thing.

Ellis: And 'I'm a no-good person for being a no-good therapist.' You see, you haven't got rid of that. So the technique in REBT is, first, *stay* with the uncomfortable situation and then *work* on the anxiety by giving up your *must*. Now, how could you give up, 'I *must* do well', 'I *have to*', 'I've *got to*'?

Yvonne: By telling myself, 'OK, I will continue, and I will try, and I will do my best, and if it works out, that will be very nice. And if it doesn't work out, well maybe I'll try another kind of er... training.'

Ellis: Or...'Maybe I'll...'

Yvonne: I'll go into another field.

Ellis: No, no...that's OK. Those are OK *practical* solutions. But better yet, 'Maybe I'll stay in this field and not *have to* be so great. It doesn't *have to* work out well – I don't *have to* do as well as the others.' Isn't that better?

Yvonne: Yes. I can be a student, a C student, and survive.

Ellis: I often talk about the Sunday painters. They're out in the park with their easels and their paints every Sunday, painting some of the most *god-awful* things, and some of them know it and they *still* enjoy painting. Now how do they *continue* to paint those *god-awful* things and still enjoy it? What are they telling themselves?

Yvonne: (1)...they *like* those god-awful things.

Ellis: Right.

Yvonne: And (2), there's nothing wrong with those god-awful things.

Ellis: Or better – there's nothing wrong with *them* for painting god-awfully. You see. And they even might say 'I don't like my paintings, but I like the *painting*.' They're doing poorly at the activity but allowing themselves to *enjoy* it. I always quote the statement of Oscar Wilde, 'Anything that's worth doing is worth doing *badly*.' You see? Because the *activity itself* is worth it. The *results* may *not* be worth it. You may never like the *results*. Now, as a therapist, we wouldn't want you to go on being a really bad therapist. And, as you said before, 'Maybe I'd better get into another field or something like that.' But that would be later when you've really determined that you're bad at therapy. First, you stay with your discomfort, as I said. Second, you recognise that you are *creating* much of it. You *make* yourself anxious. Third, you see that you mainly do it by your '*have to*', your '*got to*', your '*must*'. And by 'I am a rotten person if I do badly, rottenly.' Then you *dispute*: 'Where is the evidence that I'm a rotten person or that I *have to* do well'? And what conclusion do you end up with then?

Yvonne: I'm beginning to wonder, am I really saying that I am a rotten person or am I really and truly saying, I am a rotten therapist?

Ellis: Well, let's suppose you were. Let's suppose *that* for the moment. That would be...that might be sane. If you had enough evidence, if you did poorly time and again, and if you're not that good at therapy and you're concluding 'I am *rotten* at *therapy* and I'll never be more than average or mediocre at therapy', then that would be OK. But I doubt whether you'd withdraw from doing therapy so *quickly* if that were so.

Yvonne: Aaaah.

Ellis: You see?

Yvonne: Aaaah.

Ellis: Do you really have evidence?

Yvonne: I was going to say, I really needed evidence. I see. That I can understand.

Ellis: You see, just like those Sunday painters. They might go week after week, 52 weeks of the year, to the park and paint, and then finally say, 'You know, I like the painting but I don't like the result. Maybe I'd better do sculpture. I would get better results.' That would be OK. But if they quit after the first week then we get suspicious of their self-downing. How do they even know they're right about their *painting* but not about *themselves* being no good? You see?

Yvonne: I know you might find it very difficult to believe, but at home I have now sitting umm...some paint and some canvases [*laughing*]. Because my daughter is getting me ready for retirement. She said, 'Gee, you've always said you'd like to paint.' I have not touched the paints for two months because why? Because I know when I get to it the painting's gonna be lousy.

Ellis: And it *should* right from the start be great?

Yvonne: Be terrific! Right.

Ellis: Now isn't *that* something you're imposing on yourself? And you see it was interesting that I used painting as an example, and now it turns out that you're really in the position of copping out. But that's a good thing, because in therapy you'd at least have the excuse. 'Well if I'm rotten at therapy, I'd better not be a therapist because I might harm others.' Or something like that. But in painting, *who would you harm*? If you really work for weeks and months at it and it turned out that you were no good at it, who would be harmed? Would anybody be harmed?

Yvonne: No.

Ellis: And you would have *learned* at least the valuable information that, 'You know, painting may not *be* my cup of tea.' You would have *gathered* some evidence. Now, in cases like yours, you're withdrawing too *quickly* and therefore we probably could call it defensive. But don't accept that you are defensive because I think you are or some other therapists think you are. We could be *wrong*. You might be very perceptive and sense quickly that you're not that good at therapy and decide to do something else. That would be legitimate. But *get the evidence*. You see? And the quicker you withdraw from doing therapy the less evidence you'll have, you see?

Yvonne: Yeah, that's er…

Ellis: Anything else you wanted to raise about this?

Yvonne: No…I think that…er, this is something I really have to, er give a lot of thought to. Because it's, er…I…[*sighing*] I think this is the first time I feel that I'm down to the kernel. And, er…and I *could* do as I have done all these years, say, 'OK, terrific, that was a great session', and go out and have lunch and forget about it. But I'm gonna make myself sit on that kernel and chew on that kernel.

Ellis: That's right…

Yvonne: …And unfold. Try to unfold.

Ellis: And that's a very good point you're making. *Don't* assume that what I said was correct because I said it or because I have some status. See whether it applies to you and test it out, keep testing, you see.

Yvonne: Yeah. Uh-hum. [*Bell rings*] Was that the end?

Ellis: No. That just happened to be the bell to open the door downstairs.

Yvonne: Because I feel very well satisfied that I have gotten quite a… quite a jolt here.

Ellis: Now, how can you *use* that jolt to your benefit? That's the main thing.

Yvonne: [*sighing*]. Well, I think what I'm gonna do is sit down at home and go over the past year or so of events where I have tried to do something and er…they have not worked out…none of them has worked out and see whether indeed they have not worked out because I realistically evaluated it or er…I didn't give it enough time.

Ellis: Withdrew too quickly. Right.

Yvonne: Which was something that was brought up yesterday too er or, if…Have I given the things I have turned my hand to enough time and effort?

Ellis: Right. That's a good point.

Yvonne: Because in my case there was plenty of time, but I don't know how much effort went into these activities.

Ellis: Yeah. Because if you're telling yourself what we said before, let's just assume we're right, 'I *must* do well and isn't it awful if I don't.' And, 'If not, I might be a rotten therapist or even a rotten person.' If so, you may force yourself to continue at therapy and not really give it your *all*. So, the test of whether you're good at anything is: (1) take enough time, don't withdraw, and then (2) really throw yourself in and take it as a *challenge* to learn. You see? If you really are bad at something you still have the challenge of doing better. It's an interesting puzzle to solve if you take that attitude. Like, people don't play tick-tac-toe, because it's too easy. Some of them don't even play chequers because it is too easy, so they play chess, or Go, or some complicated game, *knowing* they're going to lose but it's a greater challenge. Now you…this is your life, let's see if you can take the *challenge* of finding out whether quitting therapy is a cop-out on your part, which we're not sure about yet, because it could be. Or whether you are quickly ascertaining whether therapy is not for you. But give it more time, give it more effort, stop musturbating* about it and then we'll see.

Yvonne: Yeah. Fine.

Ellis: You see now what you can do?

Yvonne: Yeah. That will be my homework.

Ellis: Yes. That will be your homework. To *consider* what we've said and test it as a hypothesis. It's *only* a hypothesis, and see whether you can find evidence for either your appropriately getting out of a situation, or running out pell-mell *de-fen-sive-ly*.

Yvonne: Yeah. And even as I now think, as you're talking, of the events of the past year or two, it's amazing to me that my conclusions always were 'Well, I am not, I am *not*, I am *not*' and so I dropped all of those efforts. Because I thought, 'I am *not*.'

---

*A slang term meaning holding a demand or must about something.

Ellis:	But you could have said, 'Maybe I am not. Let's see.'
Yvonne:	Yeah.
Ellis:	Right?
Yvonne:	Right.
Ellis:	OK. You work on that.
Yvonne:	Fine. Very good.
Ellis:	All right?
Yvonne:	Well, I appreciate that.

11

Commentary on Ellis's Interview with Yvonne

Ellis: OK, what problem would you like to raise?

A problem-oriented beginning from Ellis, as ever.

Yvonne: I'd like to raise something that was raised yesterday, that I thought I had, er, completely overcome.
Ellis: Yeah, what was that?
Yvonne: Well, it was pointed out to me, that I said, er: 'Well I don't torture myself any more.' I mean, that was 20 years ago I tortured myself, no more, and two of the young men in the room said: 'Is that so? Because 20 minutes ago [*laughing*] you know, I heard you torturing yourself.'
Ellis: Yeah.
Yvonne: And I thought, wow, you know. Right, I just do it in smaller bits now. I used to do it globally and, er...
Ellis: And they picked that up that you were still torturing yourself.
Yvonne: Right. And that... er...I was very disappointed.
Ellis: Because you thought that you had ended that sort of thing?
Yvonne: I thought I had conquered that.
Ellis: And they sort of brought to your attention again that you're still torturing yourself. And in what way would you say you're mainly torturing yourself now that you're looking at it?

Ellis intervenes to bring specificity to Yvonne's rather vague description of her problem.

Yvonne: Well, what brought it up, er...yesterday, was this...this whole practicum. Er...that I'm very...[*sighing*], I'm very disturbed by the fact that I don't think I do it well, that when I do the sessions with one partner that, you know, I just seem to be either floating round in the air or...or blocking, and everybody else seems to be doing so well. And this was the basis of the torture.
Ellis: So, first you *see* that they're doing better than you, you're not doing that well, and then you torture yourself, if I understand you correctly, *about* seeing that. Is that right?

Here Ellis is ensuring that he understands Yvonne's problem from her frame of reference.

Yvonne: Yes, er...but as you say, first you see I...I realise...something clicks in, and I'm evaluating it that way, I'm perceiving it that way, it doesn't necessarily have to *be* that way.

Ellis: Right. But you could perceive it and evaluate it differently. But first let's assume, because you may be exaggerating, you may not be doing *that* poorly, but let's just assume for the sake of discussion that what you're seeing, your perception, is accurate. You *are* doing poorly. Then, how do you torture yourself about that? What is your evaluation, as you just sort of indicated?

Ellis has done three things in this intervention. First, he distinguishes between perceptions (at A) and evaluations (at B). Second, he identifies Yvonne's A – that she is doing poorly – and third, he adopts the typical REBT tack at this stage – assuming temporarily that her A is true. You will note that Ellis identifies Yvonne's A a little before her C, but this is OK as there are no hard and fast rules concerning whether to assess C before A or vice versa.

Yvonne: I don't know if I would say that I torture myself. I think I, er more or less begin to say: 'Well this isn't so important anyhow and I guess I really don't wanna do this *really*, it's just taking up a week of time and that's great. It's interesting but, er...you know, it's not that important.'

Ellis: So, we would call that withdrawal. You sort of withdraw from the situation, and view it as not very important, is that right?

Yvonne: Yeah.

Ellis has found a behavioural C – withdrawal; and perhaps a defensive philosophy: 'This situation is not very important – because if I viewed it as important, I would really have to put myself down for failing at it.' While REBT therapists usually work with emotional Cs, they can and do work with behavioural Cs.

Ellis: But do you think that *underneath* that view, that 'I'm finding this not important', you're first sort of torturing yourself and therefore withdrawing. Is that your view of the torture?

Yvonne: I don't know, I'm not really, er...yeah...yeah.

Ellis: Do you think that may be going on?

Yvonne: I'm having a little trouble with defining torture.

Ellis: All right. But we can even skip torture, because we can just look at what we call C, the consequence, which would be withdrawal. So, at A, the activating event in our system of Rational Emotive Behaviour Therapy, you're perceiving that you're not

Yvonne: doing well and we're assuming, you and I, that that's true – that
    may be false, but let's assume that's true – and then at C, you
    withdraw, maybe defensively. Is that right?

Yvonne: Yes.

**Although Yvonne agrees to the C of defensive withdrawal, Ellis still
probably hypothesises that she is withdrawing from 'torture' – meaning an unhealthy negative emotion such as anxiety or depression. Also
note that the term 'torture' is very vague and probably encompasses B
and C elements. As Ellis says to Yvonne, 'torture' can be 'skipped' and her
A and C elements can be formulated using more specific referents. Note
also that in his above response Ellis is specific in mentioning A and C.
You might think that because Yvonne is a participant in a primary REBT
practicum and presumably knows what these letters refer to that this
explains why Ellis offers her no explanation. However, as we have seen
from the previous demonstration sessions, Ellis offers no such detailed
explanation to people who are not knowledgeable about REBT.**

Ellis: That maybe you're withdrawing defensively, but at least you
    withdraw. Now, what do you think you're telling yourself at B,
    to cause that withdrawal?

**Ellis once again does not explain the iB–C connection but goes straight
to assessing her irrational beliefs.**

Yvonne: OK, umm, 'I'm not as bright as I think I am', er…'These guys are
    really far more well-trained than…I am', umm, 'They're more
    perceptive than I am', 'I really have no perception…I don't
    know what the hell I'm doing', er…'I can't even drag out of a
    session the kernel of the problem, and if I'm lucky enough to
    happen on the kernel of the problem, *what do I do* ?' You know,
    er, I'm er…I don't know what to do, I don't feel schooled, or
    trained, or…or able, umm, to *be* a therapist.

**Note that Yvonne does not offer irrational beliefs in response to Ellis's
open-ended enquiry. Rather, she comes up with further inferences at A
(or what in his next response Ellis refers to as observations). This is
quite a common response from clients to such open-ended enquiries. If
Ellis had asked a theory-driven question such as 'What do you think
you were demanding about not doing well that led to your withdrawal?' Yvonne might have provided her irrational belief. As the term
implies, a theory-driven question is a question informed by REBT theory,
'What were you demanding?' rather than the more open-ended 'What
were you telling yourself?'**

Ellis: Right. Those are all observations that you're making about your
    performance compared with their performance. 'I'm not bright

Yvonne: enough', 'I'm not well-schooled enough', 'I seem to be confused about what to do'; is that right?

Yvonne: Yes.

Ellis: You're observing those things about your performance compared with *their* performance.

Yvonne: Well, I thought I was feeling those things.

Ellis: Well, but at first; isn't there an observation that that's what you see? We'll get to the feeling in a minute, and we know the behaviour to a certain degree already: you're withdrawing. But once you perceive those things, and let's just assume the worst – we like to assume the worst in REBT just to show people that they can go with even the worst – so, let's assume you're accurate, you're quite accurate, that compared with them you are below par and that as a therapist compared with them again you're not so hot. That's what you're perceiving and evaluating, you're right, you are evaluating that. But *that* kind of observation and evaluation of performance wouldn't make you withdraw. Do you know why it wouldn't make you withdraw if you only stuck with that kind of observation and evaluation: why wouldn't you withdraw?

Here Ellis does a number of things. First, he helps Yvonne to distinguish between her perceptions (or what I call inferences) and her feelings. Second, he reminds Yvonne that they are still assuming that her A is true. Finally, he distinguishes between perceptions and evaluations of performance (which properly belong at A) and a more central type of evaluation that explains her withdrawal and that constitutes irrational beliefs at B (as we shall soon see).

Yvonne: Possibly because I see others who are equally inept.

Ellis: That would be one thing. That's right. You see others who are inept. But also you could conclude: 'Even though this is so, I'm glad I now see that. Maybe I'd better throw myself into it more and get more training and overcome these deficiencies.' Couldn't that be a legitimate conclusion?

Yvonne: Yes…yes.

Ellis: And then you wouldn't withdraw.

Yvonne: Right.

Ellis: But we know that you *did* feel like withdrawing. Right?

Yvonne: Yes.

Ellis: That's your feeling: 'I don't wanna be here. I'd better withdraw.' Now, therefore, we believe in REBT that there's an additional evaluation. In addition to the evaluation of your performance, you're saying something *stronger* about *it* and about *you*. Now, if I'm right about that, and I could be wrong but I'm just hypothesising now, what would you be saying that's *stronger* that would make you withdraw?

Again, Ellis is adopting an open-ended rather than a theory-driven enquiry to help Yvonne discover her irrational beliefs at B.

Yvonne: If I continue I'm gonna make a real ass of myself.

Ellis: And if I make an ass of myself...

Yvonne: If I make a real ass of myself [*laughing*], it's another notch in my belt of asshood.

Ellis: Right. And that proves *what* about you?

Yvonne: That I will die an ass.

Ellis: I will *always* be an ass, I'm a hopeless ass do you mean, or something like that?

Yvonne: I am never going to er...I am never going to get it all straightened out.

Ellis: Right. Now, do you see then, that you have two sets of observations and evaluations? The first one, merely 'Compared with them I'm not doing well, and maybe I never will.' And that *might* be true, you see. It could be that you're just evaluating correctly, that your performance is never going to be up to theirs. But *then* you say: 'My performance makes me an ass and a hopeless ass and I'll *die* an ass as I *live* an ass,' is that right?

Here Ellis helps Yvonne to discriminate keenly between her self-depreciating irrational belief and her evaluation of performance at A.

Yvonne: Yes.

Ellis: Now *that's* the evaluation...

Yvonne: [*laughing*] My God, that sounds terrible.

Yvonne's last statement indicates that she probably has a meta-emotional problem – that she feels 'terrible' about her negative evaluation of herself. Note that Ellis does not address this here and in fact does not return to this meta-emotional problem in this interview. Sometimes, Ellis deals with meta-emotional problems as soon as they are revealed, at other times he deals with them later and occasionally, as here, he does not deal with them at all. The reasons behind his clinical decisions on this issue are not apparent from his in-session behaviour. My guess is that Ellis probably does not want to lose the momentum that he has achieved at this point of the interview and thus he keeps his focus on Yvonne's primary problem, her self-depreciation because of her perceived inefficiency as a therapist.

Ellis: That's right, you see. And that's what we want to question, and that's why we go to D, disputing. Let's suppose the worst again, that your observation is true and let's even suppose you go *on* acting this way, you're not very good at therapy as they are. How does that make you, a human, an ass?

Ellis could question Yvonne's perception of herself being inefficacious as a therapist, but instead he goes forward to the more elegant solution of REBT – even if she can provide evidence of this inefficiency how does that prove that she, an entire person, is an ass?

Also, note that Ellis does not formally help Yvonne to connect her irrational belief with her withdrawal at C. Remember that he tends not to do this in demonstration sessions, whereas other REBT therapists, including myself, would. Consequently as soon as Yvonne reveals her irrational belief, Ellis disputes it.

Yvonne: I guess somewhere I feel that I *have to* excel at *something*.

It is interesting to note that as soon as Ellis disputes Yvonne's self-depreciation belief, she comes up with her musturbatory belief.

Ellis: Right. You see the '*have to*'.
Yvonne: I *have to* excel at something.
Ellis: And if you change that '*have to*', to 'I'd *like to* excel at something, but if I don't, I don't', would you then feel like an ass?
Yvonne: No, I wouldn't. But I really have to change the whole statement anyway. I *have to* excel at *everything*. I want to excel at *everything* I touch.
Ellis: Well, but you notice you just said two things. I *want to* excel at everything', which I think almost every human says, 'I'd *like to*', 'I *want to* excel at all *important* things'. Not tiddly-winks, you don't care if you don't excel at tiddly-winks, do you?
Yvonne: No, that would be all right. *That* would show that I was only human.
Ellis: Yes, right. But you want to excel at every important thing and then you say 'and therefore I *have to*', is that right?
Yvonne: Yes.
Ellis: Now, in REBT we never question desires, preferences, wishes, wants, because you could *want* anything. You could want, right now, 10 million dollars, or to be the greatest genius at therapy in the world, and as long as you were saying 'I *want to*, but I don't *have to*', you wouldn't be into trouble. But we question the '*have to*'. Why *must* you excel at an important thing like therapy? Why must you?

Ellis takes care in helping Yvonne to see the difference between what I call her full preference (which contains an asserted preference component – 'I want to' – and a negated demand component – '...but I don't have to') and her demand (see Chapter 1 and Dryden, 2001).

Yvonne: I don't know.
Ellis: Well, think about that.

Ellis could easily tell her the 'right' answer here. But he prefers that she figure it out herself.

Yvonne: Well, I dunno. I suppose…er…I think it may be that I'm a product of growing up where I've been told, or it's been implied that if you do something, do it well.

Yvonne doesn't directly respond to Ellis's disputing question: 'Why must you excel at an important thing like therapy?' Note how Ellis responds in this next intervention.

Ellis: Right. Let's suppose that's true. And, incidentally, that has sense to it, because if you do something well, it would be *preferable* to doing it poorly. We all learn that because that's not false. Our parents and our schools and our books teach us to try to do well. 'If at once you don't succeed, try try again to succeed.' Isn't that what it means? And so that's OK. But we're still asking another question, not why it's *preferable* to do well, why *must* you do what's preferable? Why do you *have to*?

Ellis shows Yvonne that her answer to his previous question provides evidence of why it is preferable to do well. Then he asks her why she must do what is preferable. Again, this is a typical Ellis intervention.

Yvonne: I feel better when I…when I *do* accomplish. I feel better about myself.

Ellis: Ah, about *yourself*. But you see you've just again said two things, (1) 'I feel better about *it*', which we hope is true – that you would feel better about accomplishment rather than sitting on your rump and doing nothing or doing badly. So you'd better feel better about it. But you're saying 'I feel better about *me*, I only accept *me* when I do *it* well.' Now, is *that* a legitimate conclusion? 'I can only accept *me, myself*, my *being*, my *totality* when I do *it*, therapy, well.' Now is that a good conclusion?

Ellis tracks Yvonne quite carefully here. You will note that he originally disputed her self-depreciation belief, moved to disputing her demanding belief when she moved to this type of irrational belief (iB) and has now gone back to disputing her self-depreciation belief. My own preference is to help the client to dispute fully one type of iB before moving to a related iB. Thus, I might have helped Yvonne to dispute her self-depreciation belief more fully before disputing her must.

Yvonne: You mean, is it accurate?
Ellis: Well, will it give you good results?

You will note that Yvonne and Ellis refer to the three criteria for irrationality – empirical, logical and pragmatic – in very quick succession. My preference here would have been to slow the pace down so that Yvonne could have considered more fully each criterion in turn.

Yvonne: No, it won't give me good results.

Ellis: It'll give you what you have…withdrawal, anxiety. Maybe what you said at the beginning of this session, some kind of anguish, terror almost, which may be the thing that is making you withdraw – which we could just guess about, but it certainly *won't give you pleasure* and it won't help you to stay with this practicum or any other thing that you enter. You'll tend to run away. And by running away will you do as well as you'd like to do?

Yvonne: No.

Ellis: You'll normally do worse, isn't that so?

Yvonne: Well, I will not have accomplished anything at all.

Ellis: That's right.

Yvonne: Except to have reinforced again, once again, Yvonne strikes out.

Ellis: That's the irony, you see. That's really an irony. By demanding that 'I must do "X" well', such as therapy in a practicum. '*I have to*', '*I have to*', '*I've got to*', '*I've got to* do it well', you will withdraw and not even do it *at all*. You see the *need*, the *necessity* of performing well leads to withdrawal or anxiety which interferes with your performance. You see that's catch-22. Now, how do you think you can get out of that bind?

You will note that Ellis focuses on pragmatic disputing of Yvonne's irrational beliefs in this sequence.

Yvonne: By not withdrawing and not being anxious.

Ellis: That's right. First, not withdrawing. Then you still would be anxious if you didn't withdraw. Now, how could you get rid of your anxiety? Let's assume you stayed with it, and it was *uncomfortable* to stay. And that's what we recommend in REBT, to stay with your discomfort until you make yourself comfortable. How could you get rid of the anxiety by staying with your discomfort?

Yvonne: By applying myself more, and er…learning the techniques.

Ellis: Right. That's one way, but that's a little inelegant. That would work, because let's suppose that you stayed with it no matter how uncomfortable you felt and you learned the techniques of doing therapy. You got better at it and you felt *un-anxious*. Do you realise why that would be an inelegant kind of solution? It would work, temporarily, but why would it only work temporarily? Why would it be inelegant?

By using Socratic questioning, Ellis is attempting to get Yvonne to see that the only elegant way of overcoming her withdrawal and the anxiety that underpins her defensive behaviour is to challenge and change her irrational beliefs. He makes this point more explicitly in his next response but one.

Yvonne: Because I think it attacks just a very small piece of it.

Ellis: That's right. And even in that small piece, suppose you first did well, and then later did badly. Suppose you finished the practicum, learned REBT quite well, as well as anybody does, and then compare yourself with other therapists and *still* do poorly. Then what would you go back to telling yourself?

Yvonne: That I really don't belong here. I'll go back to the same thing.

Ellis: And 'I'm a no-good person for being a no-good therapist.' You see, you haven't got rid of that. So the technique in REBT is, first, *stay* with the uncomfortable situation and then *work* on the anxiety by giving up your *must*. Now, how could you give up, 'I *must* do well', 'I *have to*', 'I've *got to*'?

Ellis doesn't merely encourage Yvonne to act well by staying in the uncomfortable therapy situation, he wants her to do that and to tackle her must – to think differently and act differently.

Yvonne: By telling myself, 'OK, I will continue, and I will try, and I will do my best, and if it works out, that will be very nice. And if it doesn't work out, well maybe I'll try another kind of er... training.'

Ellis: Or...'Maybe I'll...'

Yvonne: I'll go into another field.

Ellis: No, no...that's OK. Those are OK *practical* solutions. But better yet, 'Maybe I'll stay in this field and not *have to* be so great. It doesn't *have to* work out well – I don't *have to* do as well as the others.' Isn't that better?

Yvonne doesn't fully see that the real psychological solution to her emotional problem is to challenge and change her must. So Ellis emphasises this solution without denigrating her more practically oriented solutions.

Yvonne: Yes. I can be a student, a C student, and survive.

Ellis: I often talk about the Sunday painters. They're out in the park with their easels and their paints every Sunday, painting some of the most *god-awful* things, and some of them know it and they *still* enjoy painting. Now how do they *continue* to paint those *god-awful* things and still enjoy it? What are they telling themselves?

Here Ellis is using a metaphor to reinforce his point (see DiGiuseppe, 1991b).

Yvonne: (1)... they *like* those god-awful things.

Ellis: Right.

Yvonne: And (2), there's nothing wrong with those god-awful things.

Ellis: Or better – there's nothing wrong with *them* for painting god-awfully. You see. And they even might say 'I don't like my paintings, but I like the *painting*.' They're doing poorly at the activity but allowing themselves to *enjoy* it. I always quote the statement of Oscar Wilde, 'Anything that's worth doing is worth doing *badly*.' You see? Because the *activity itself* is worth it. The *results* may *not* be worth it. You may never like the *results*. Now, as a therapist, we wouldn't want you to go on being a really bad therapist. And, as you said before, 'Maybe I'd better get into another field or something like that.' But that would be later when you've really determined that you're bad at therapy. First, you stay with your discomfort, as I said. Second, you recognise that you are *creating* much of it. You *make* yourself anxious. Third, you see that you mainly do it by your *'have to'*, your *'got to'*, your *'must'*. And by 'I am a rotten person if I do badly, rottenly.' Then you *dispute*: 'Where is the evidence that I'm a rotten person or that I *have to* do well'? And what conclusion do you end up with then?

Ellis persists in trying to help Yvonne get to her core dysfunctional belief – that she must be good at therapy and is a rotten person if she does not do as well as she must.

Yvonne: I'm beginning to wonder, am I really saying that I am a rotten person or am I really and truly saying, I am a rotten therapist?

Ellis: Well, let's suppose you were. Let's suppose *that* for the moment. That would be...that might be sane. If you had enough evidence, if you did poorly time and again, and if you're not that good at therapy and you're concluding 'I am *rotten* at *therapy* and I'll never be more than average or mediocre at therapy', then that would be OK. But I doubt whether you'd withdraw from doing therapy so *quickly* if that were so.

Yvonne: Aaaah.

Ellis: You see?

Yvonne: Aaaah.

Ellis: Do you really have evidence?

Yvonne: I was going to say, I really needed evidence. I see. That I can understand.

Ellis: You see, just like those Sunday painters. They might go week after week, 52 weeks of the year, to the park and paint, and then finally say, 'You know, I like the painting but I don't like the result. Maybe I'd better do sculpture. I would get better results.' That would be OK. But if they quit after the first week then we get suspicious of their self-downing. How do they even know they're right about their *painting* but not about *themselves* being no good? You see?

By continuing to use the Sunday painter metaphor, Ellis helps Yvonne to see that her defensive withdrawal prevents her from identifying, challenging and changing her irrational beliefs.

Yvonne: I know you might find it very difficult to believe, but at home I have now sitting umm…some paint and some canvases [*laughing*]. Because my daughter is getting me ready for retirement. She said, 'Gee, you've always said you'd like to paint.' I have not touched the paints for two months because why? Because I know when I get to it the painting's gonna be lousy.

Ellis: And it *should* right from the start be great?

Yvonne: Be terrific! Right.

Ellis: Now isn't *that* something you're imposing on yourself? And you see it was interesting that I used painting as an example, and now it turns out that you're really in the position of copping out. But that's a good thing, because in therapy you'd at least have the excuse. 'Well if I'm rotten at therapy, I'd better not be a therapist because I might harm others.' Or something like that. But in painting, *who would you harm*? If you really work for weeks and months at it and it turned out that you were no good at it, who would be harmed? Would anybody be harmed?

Ellis now helps Yvonne to begin to generalise her learning about the role of her irrational beliefs from the therapy situation to painting.

Yvonne: No.

Ellis: And you would have *learned* at least the valuable information that, 'You know, painting may not *be* my cup of tea.' You would have *gathered* some evidence. Now, in cases like yours, you're withdrawing too *quickly* and therefore we probably could call it defensive. But don't accept that you are defensive because I think you are or some other therapists think you are. We could be *wrong*. You might be very perceptive and sense quickly that you're not that good at therapy and decide to do something else. That would be legitimate. But *get the evidence*. You see? And the quicker you withdraw from doing therapy the less evidence you'll have, you see?

Ellis is using evidence and logic here to try to show Yvonne that she is not necessarily wrong to withdraw from therapy but that her

withdrawing so quickly tends to show that she may be avoiding self-depreciation about her feeling. He is not trying to prove that she is defensively withdrawing but only that she may be. His interpretation could be wrong, and he doesn't foist it on her. An important part of REBT is encouraging clients to think for themselves and not to accept what their therapists say simply because they are therapists.

Yvonne: Yeah, that's er…

Ellis: Anything else you wanted to raise about this?

Yvonne: No…I think that…er, this is something I really have to, er give a lot of thought to. Because it's, er… I… [*sighing*] I think this is the first time I feel that I'm down to the kernel. And, er…and I *could* do as I have done all these years, say, 'OK, terrific, that was a great session', and go out and have lunch and forget about it. But I'm gonna make myself sit on that kernel and chew on that kernel.

Ellis: That's right…

Yvonne: …And unfold. Try to unfold.

Ellis: And that's a very good point you're making. *Don't* assume that what I said was correct because I said it or because I have some status. See whether it applies to you and test it out, keep testing, you see.

Yvonne: Yeah. Uh-hum. [*Bell rings*] Was that the end?

Ellis: No. That just happened to be the bell to open the door downstairs.

Yvonne: Because I feel very well satisfied that I have gotten quite a…quite a jolt here.

Ellis: Now, how can you use that jolt to your benefit? That's the main thing.

No matter how much insight Yvonne seems to be getting, Ellis wants to make sure that she uses it to work against her self-depreciation, her defensiveness and her withdrawal, and her basic musts that lie behind these feelings and actions, and to change them.

Yvonne: [*sighing*] Well, I think what I'm gonna do is sit down at home and go over the past year or so of events where I have tried to do something and er…they have not worked out…none of them has worked out and see whether indeed they have not worked out because I realistically evaluated it or er…I didn't give it enough time.

Yvonne suggests to herself a homework assignment to test for herself the validity of Ellis's hypothesis. Ellis thus does not need to make the point that one way in which she can deepen her learning is by the use of homework assignments.

Ellis: Withdrew too quickly. Right.

Yvonne: Which was something that was brought up yesterday too er or, if…Have I given the things I have turned my hand to enough time and effort?

Ellis: Right. That's a good point.

Yvonne: Because in my case there was plenty of time, but I don't know how much effort went into these activities.

Ellis: Yeah. Because if you're telling yourself what we said before, let's just assume we're right, 'I *must* do well and isn't it awful if I don't.' And, 'If not, I might be a rotten therapist or even a rotten person.' If so, you may force yourself to continue at therapy and not really give it your *all*. So, the test of whether you're good at anything is: (1) take enough time, don't withdraw, and then (2) really throw yourself in and take it as a *challenge* to learn. You see? If you really are bad at something you still have the challenge of doing better. It's an interesting puzzle to solve if you take that attitude. Like, people don't play tick-tac-toe, because it's too easy. Some of them don't even play chequers because it is too easy, so they play chess, or Go, or some complicated game, *knowing* they're going to lose but it's a greater challenge. Now you…this is your life, let's see if you can take the *challenge* of finding out whether quitting therapy is a cop-out on your part, which we're not sure about yet, because it could be. Or whether you are quickly ascertaining whether therapy is not for you. But give it more time, give it more effort, stop musturbating* about it and then we'll see.

Ellis does not want her immediately to stop doing therapy – or to decide to continue doing it. He would like her to consider the hypotheses they discussed about her history of failing and about her consequently defensive withdrawal. He hopes that she will experiment more, without musturbating, to see what her final conclusion about being a therapist might be.

Yvonne: Yeah. Fine.

Ellis: You see now what you can do?

Yvonne: Yeah. That will be my homework.

Ellis: Yes. That will be your homework. To *consider* what we've said and test it as a hypothesis. It's *only* a hypothesis, and see whether you can find evidence for either your appropriately getting out of a situation, or running out pell-mell *de-fen-sive-ly*.

Yvonne: Yeah. And even as I now think, as you're talking, of the events of the past year or two, it's amazing to me that my conclusions always were 'Well, I am not, I am *not*, I am *not*' and so I dropped all of those efforts. Because I thought, 'I am *not*.'

---

*A slang term meaning holding a demand or must about something.

Ellis: But you could have said, 'Maybe I am not. Let's see.'
Yvonne: Yeah.
Ellis: Right?
Yvonne: Right.
Ellis: OK. You work on that.
Yvonne: Fine. Very good.
Ellis: All right?
Yvonne: Well, I appreciate that.

References

DiGiuseppe, R. (1991a). A rational-emotive model of assessment. In M.E. Bernard (Ed.), *Using rational-emotive therapy effectively*. New York: Plenum.

DiGiuseppe, R. (1991b). Comprehensive cognitive disputing in RET. In M.E. Bernard (Ed.), *Using rational-emotive therapy effectively*. New York: Plenum.

DiGiuseppe, R., Leaf, R., & Linscott, J. (1993). The therapeutic relationship in rational-emotive therapy: Some preliminary data. *Journal of Rational-Emotive & Cognitive-Behavior Therapy, 11,* 223–233.

Dryden, W. (1998a). Understanding persons in the context of their problems: A rational emotive behaviour therapy perspective. In M. Bruch & F.W. Bond (Eds), *Beyond diagnosis: Case formulation approaches in CBT*. Chichester: Wiley.

Dryden, W. (1998b). *Are you sitting uncomfortably?: Windy Dryden, live and uncut*. Ross-on-Wye: PCCS Books.

Dryden, W. (2001). *Reason to change: A rational emotive behaviour therapy (REBT) workbook*. Hove: Brunner-Routledge.

Dryden, W. (Ed.) (2002). *Idiosyncratic rational emotive behaviour therapy*. Ross-on-Wye: PCCS Books.

Dryden, W., Backx, W., & Ellis, A. (2002). Problems in living : The Friday Night Workshop. In W. Dryden & M. Neenan (Eds), *Rational emotive behaviour group therapy*. London: Whurr.

Ellis, A. (1963). Toward a more precise definition of 'emotional' and 'intellectual' insight. *Psychological Reports, 13,* 125–126.

Ellis, A. (1979). Rejoinder: Elegant and inelegant RET. In A. Ellis & J.M. Whiteley (Eds), *Theoretical and empirical foundations of rational-emotive therapy*. Monterey, CA: Brooks/Cole.

Ellis, A. (1985). Dilemmas of giving warmth or love to clients. In W. Dryden, *Therapists' dilemmas*. London: Harper & Row.

Ellis, A. (1989). Ineffective consumerism in the cognitive-behaviour therapies and in general psychotherapy. In W. Dryden & P. Trower (Eds), *Cognitive psychotherapy: stasis and change*. London: Cassell.

Ellis, A., & Dryden, W. (1997). *The practice of rational emotive behavior therapy*. (2nd ed.). New York: Springer.

Ellis, A., & Joffe, D. (2002). A study of volunteer clients who experienced live sessions of rational emotive behavior therapy in front of a public audience. *Journal of Rational-Emotive & Cognitive-Behavior Therapy, 20,* 151–158.

Rogers, C.R. (1957). The necessary and sufficient conditions of therapeutic personality change. *Journal of Consulting Psychology, 21,* 95–103.

Shostrom, E.L. (Producer) (1965). *Three approaches to psychotherapy* (Part 3 – Albert Ellis) [film]. Orange, CA: Psychological Films.

Weinrach, S.G. (1986). Ellis and Gloria: Positive or negative model. *Psychotherapy: Theory, Research and Practice, 23,* 642–648.

Yankura, J., & Dryden, W. (1990). *Doing RET: Albert Ellis in action*. New York: Springer.

Index